Dermot F. Reynolds

Open for Business

WORKBOOK

Gill & Macmillan

Published in Ireland by
Gill & Macmillan
with associated companies throughout the world
www.gillmacmillan.ie

© Dermot F. Reynolds 2010
978 07171 47458

Design and typesetting by webucation.ie

Contents

eTest.ie – what is it?

A revolutionary new website-based testing platform that facilitates a social learning environment for Irish schools. Both students and teachers can use it, either independently or together, to make the whole area of testing easier, more engaging and more productive for all.

Students – do you want to know how well you are doing? Then take an eTest!

At eTest.ie, you can access tests put together by the author of this textbook. You get instant results, so they're a brilliant way to quickly check just how your study or revision is going.

Since each eTest is based on your textbook, if you don't know an answer, you'll find it in your book.

Register now and you can save all of your eTest results to use as a handy revision aid or to simply compare with your friends' results!

Teachers – eTest.ie will engage your students and help them with their revision, while making the jobs of reviewing their progress and homework easier and more convenient for all of you.

Register now to avail of these exciting features:

- Create tests easily using our pre-set questions OR you can create your own questions

- Develop your own online learning centre for each class that you teach

- Keep track of your students' performances

eTest.ie has a wide choice of question types for you to choose from, most of which can be graded automatically, like multiple-choice, jumbled-sentence, matching, ordering and gap-fill exercises. This free resource allows you to create class groups, delivering all the functionality of a VLE (Virtual Learning Environment) with the ease of communication that is brought by social networking.

Chapter 1

Understanding *income*

1 Find the different types of income hidden in this grid:

Wages ✓

Salaries

Overtime

Interest

Commission

Pension

Bonus

Benefit

S	E	R	W	S	N	T	U	N	O	B
I	M	P	O	E	T	R	E	S	V	O
S	I	E	L	V	R	S	E	A	M	M
B	O	N	U	S	E	G	W	L	A	G
E	P	S	E	N	A	R	S	A	O	N
N	T	I	R	W	E	S	T	R	M	T
E	C	O	M	M	I	S	S	I	O	N
F	A	N	O	I	S	N	E	E	M	C
I	C	I	N	T	E	R	E	S	T	E
T	S	E	G	W	A	R	E	V	O	B

2 Tick (✓) whether the following income items are regular or additional:

	REGULAR	ADDITIONAL
Wages		
Overtime		
Jobseeker's benefit		
Sales commission		
Bonus		

3 What do the following letters stand for? *(Write **each** answer in full in the space provided.)*

PAYE	
PRSI	

4 In each space below, write the most appropriate word or term from the following list:

TOTAL DEDUCTIONS   PENSION   BASIC PAY   GROSS PAY   OVERTIME

(Two of the words/terms above do not complete any of the sentences below.)

(i) Gross pay equals .... plus ....

(ii) Net pay equals.............................. minus.............................. .

5 Explain the term **Fringe Benefit**:

....

....

....

....

6 Find a word or phrase in the list to complete the words in the table:

in kind

bonus

vouchers

expenses

benefit

travelling	
jobseeker's	
Christmas	
luncheon	
benefits	

7 Column 1 is a list of words and phrases. Column 2 is a list of descriptions which can be matched to these words and phrases. *(One description cannot be matched.)*

Column 1	Column 2
Words and phrases	**Descriptions**

1. Perk	A. Income for retired people
2. Net income	B. A non-statutory deduction
3. Overtime	C. A statutory deduction
4. Pension	D. A fringe benefit
5. Bonus	E. Money paid to sales people
6. Commission	F. Work a person does outside normal hours
7. PAYE	G. Reduce the amount of tax you have to pay
8. Tax credits	H. Take-home pay
9. Gross wages	I. Money given to you by your parents
10. Union dues	J. Income before any deductions
	K. Additional income sometimes given at Christmas or summer

Match the two lists by placing the letter of the most appropriate description under the relevant number below:

1.	2.	3.	4.	5.	6.	7.	8.	9.	10.

8 Tick (✓) whether each of the following are fringe benefits:

	TRUE	FALSE
Travelling allowance		
Wages		
Luncheon vouchers		
Clothing allowance		
Salary		
Christmas bonus		
Use of photocopier for personal reasons		
Loans at low interest rate		
Jobseeker's benefit		
Use of social facilities		

ARE WE PAYING TOO MUCH PAYE/PRSI?

TOO MANY DEDUCTIONS – TOO FEW BENEFITS

By Carol Dillon

Audrey is married to Liam and they have two children. They both work. Audrey works in the office of a printing company in town. "I am paid €650 wages each week," she says, "and when I work overtime I earn another €150." Her employer also gives her €20 luncheon vouchers each week that she can use in local cafés. As she works in the office she can use the Internet or phone home when she is not busy.

Her husband, Liam, is a sales rep for a medical company. He has a company car and drives about 30,000 miles each year visiting hospitals. "I get paid 20% commission on all my sales," he says. When he visits a hospital he gives staff free company pens and no one seems to mind when he keeps a few himself. If the business is doing well he gets a €500 bonus at Christmas.

A few years ago Liam's father died and his mother, Mary, came to live with them. Every Friday she walks to the Post Office to collect her €120 old-age pension and then she uses her bus pass to go to town. Once a year at Christmas she withdraws the interest on her savings in the Post Office.

Audrey and Liam do not get to keep all the money they earn. Their employers must first deduct PAYE and PRSI from their wages. In addition Audrey pays €4 union dues each week and Liam pays VHI. Sometimes they complain about the deductions. "Why do they take so much?" Audrey says. "I don't mind paying union dues because I know the union will help me if I need it, but what benefit do I get from paying PAYE and PRSI?"

9 **Scan the information in the article above.**

The following figures are mentioned. What do they relate to?

€650	
€150	
€20	
30,000	
20%	
€500	
€120	
€4	

10 Read the article on the previous page and answer these questions.

Which person can earn overtime?

....

Which person earns commission?

....

Which person gets a pension?

....

Why do they not get to keep all the money they earn?

....

....

What does the government do with the PAYE it collects?

....

....

What is the PRSI money used for?

....

....

11 Read the article on the previous page and complete this table:

		Audrey	Liam	Mary
INCOME	Regular			
	Additional			
PERKS	Official			
	Unofficial			
DEDUCTIONS	Statutory			
	Non-statutory			

12 | **Wages Slip:** EMMA CLEARY | | | | **Week:** 12

PAY	€	DEDUCTIONS	€	NET PAY
Basic	576.00	PAYE	132.00	
Overtime	72.00	PRSI	35.00	**€466.00**
		VHI	15.00	
GROSS PAY	648.00	**TOTAL DEDUCTIONS**	182.00	

Study Emma's payslip for last week above and answer these questions:

(a) How much overtime did Emma earn?

(b) What are her total earnings this week?

(c) How much tax did she pay?

(d) How much does she pay for health insurance?

(e) How much is her take-home pay?

13 Activity 1.2

Complete payslips for each of the following:

1 Shane Tracy, basic pay €160, overtime €20, PAYE €8, PRSI €3, union dues €3.

Wages Slip:				Week:
PAY	€	DEDUCTIONS	€	NET PAY
Basic		PAYE		
Overtime		PRSI		€
		Union dues		
GROSS PAY		**TOTAL DEDUCTIONS**		

2 Linda Tierney, basic pay €330, overtime €50, PAYE €47, PRSI €16, Quinn Healthcare €20.

Wages Slip:				Week:
PAY	€	DEDUCTIONS	€	NET PAY
Basic		PAYE		
Overtime		PRSI		€
		Quinn Healthcare		
GROSS PAY		**TOTAL DEDUCTIONS**		

3   Kevin O'Neill, basic pay €570, overtime €60, PAYE €97, PRSI €30, pension €50.

Wages Slip:			Week:	
PAY	**€**	**DEDUCTIONS**	**€**	**NET PAY**
Basic		PAYE		
Overtime		PRSI		**€**
		Pension		
GROSS PAY		**TOTAL DEDUCTIONS**		

4   Sinead Ryan, basic pay €700, overtime €100, PAYE €131, PRSI €35, union dues €5.

Wages Slip:			Week:	
PAY	**€**	**DEDUCTIONS**	**€**	**NET PAY**
Basic		PAYE		
Overtime		PRSI		**€**
		Union dues		
GROSS PAY		**TOTAL DEDUCTIONS**		

5   Brendan Doyle, basic pay €200, overtime €80, PAYE €27, PRSI €15, VHI €20.

Wages Slip:			Week:	
PAY	**€**	**DEDUCTIONS**	**€**	**NET PAY**
Basic		PAYE		
Overtime		PRSI		**€**
		VHI		
GROSS PAY		**TOTAL DEDUCTIONS**		

Extra payslip

Wages Slip:			Week:	
PAY	**€**	**DEDUCTIONS**	**€**	**NET PAY**
Basic		PAYE		
Overtime		PRSI		**€**
GROSS PAY		**TOTAL DEDUCTIONS**		

14 Study the following cash account for a working couple and answer the true/false questions:

Dr							Cr
Date	Details	F	Total	Date	Details	F	Total
Nov			€	Nov			€
2	Balance		70	2	Telephone		90
3	Wages		650	3	Supermarket		110
4	Wages		820	4	Mortgage		700
				5	Petrol		34
				6	Suit		199

Cash Account

	TRUE	FALSE
They had €70 from last week to spend this week		
They earned €1,470 in total this week		
Total expenditure is €1,133 this week		
They have €407 left at the end of this week		

(Tick (✓) the most appropriate box.)

15 Complete a cash account for Mr and Mrs Foley using this information:

April   1 Cash on hand €120

         2 Mr Foley received his wages €740

         3 Paid supermarket €110

         4 Paid butcher €26

         5 Mrs Foley received her wages €720

         5 Paid light and heat bill €90

         6 Paid mortgage €650

eTest.ie
Try a test on this topic

Dr							Cr
Date	Details	F	Total	Date	Details	F	Total
			€				€

Cash Account

Chapter 2

Personal *expenditure*

1 What do the following letters stand for? *(Write **each** answer in full in the space provided.)*

DD	
SO	

2 Tick (✓) whether the following income items are capital or current expenditure:

	CAPITAL	CURRENT
Buying a dishwasher		
Buying tablets for the dishwasher		
Buying a printer for your computer		
Buying paper for the printer		
Buying a scooter		
Buying petrol for the scooter		

3 Find a word in the list to complete the terms in the table:

ORDER

OPPORTUNITY

EXPENDITURE

DIRECT

	DEBIT
STANDING	
	COST
CAPITAL	

4 Explain the term **Opportunity Cost**:

....

....

....

....

2 Monday
Bought milk, bread, jam and butter €4.50.
Hope to buy new shoes on Thursday in town.

5 Thursday
Bought milk, tissues and pizza €6.30. Bought the shoes €120.

3 Tuesday
Bought milk, ham and eggs €7.80.

6 Friday
Started my new diet today. Bought milk, water, fruit, lettuce and tomatoes €5.40.

4 Wednesday
Bought milk, bread, steak and chips €8.70.
Had a headache all day and went to the doctor €50.

7 Saturday
Bought milk, fruit and could not resist cakes €5.90.

8 Sunday
Bought milk and went out for dinner €23. So much for the diet!

5 Study Sally's diary above and identify (you may use the same item more than once if you like):

(a) one fixed expenditure item	
(b) one irregular expenditure item	
(c) one discretionary expenditure item	
(e) one impulse purchase	
(f) one item of capital expenditure	
(g) one item of current expenditure	
What is her total expenditure for the week?	

6 Explain the term **Impulse Buying**:

....

....

....

....

7 Column 1 is a list of words and phrases. Column 2 is a list of descriptions which can be matched to these words and phrases. *(One description cannot be matched.)*

Column 1	Column 2
Words and phrases	**Descriptions**

1. Impulse purchase
2. Debit
3. Analysed
4. Fixed expenditure
5. Capital expenditure
6. Irregular expenditure
7. Opportunity cost
8. Mortgage
9. Discretionary expenses
10. Credit

A. Expenses that follow a pattern
B. The cost of the alternatives
C. The left-hand side of the cash account
D. Spending on luxuries
E. Something you did not plan to buy
F. A loan to buy a house
G. Buying petrol for the car
H. Broken up into different parts
I. Expenses that do not follow a pattern
J. The right-hand side of the cash account
K. Buying a car

Match the two lists by placing the letter of the most appropriate description under the relevant number below:

1.	2.	3.	4.	5.	6.	7.	8.	9.	10.

8 The following are meter readings taken from an electricity bill. Calculate the number of units used **and** the total charge. Enter your answers in the appropriate spaces.

Electricity Meter Readings		Workings
Present	57430	
Previous	56580	
No. of units used		
Rate per unit	€0.20	
Total charge	€	

9 Complete analysed cash accounts for Mr and Mrs Byrne for April. In each case the expenses are grouped using the following headings:

Income: Total

Expenditure: Total, Household, Light and heat, Car, Other.

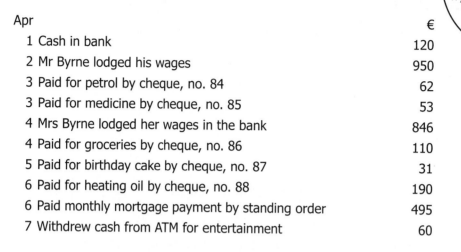

Apr		€
1	Cash in bank	120
2	Mr Byrne lodged his wages	950
3	Paid for petrol by cheque, no. 84	62
3	Paid for medicine by cheque, no. 85	53
4	Mrs Byrne lodged her wages in the bank	846
4	Paid for groceries by cheque, no. 86	110
5	Paid for birthday cake by cheque, no. 87	31
6	Paid for heating oil by cheque, no. 88	190
6	Paid monthly mortgage payment by standing order	495
7	Withdrew cash from ATM for entertainment	60

Dr			Analysed Cash Account								Cr
Date	Details	F	Total	Date	Details	F	Total	Household	Light and heat	Car	Other
			€				€	€	€	€	€

Chapter 3
Household *budget*

1   Tick (✓) whether the following expenses are fixed, irregular or discretionary:

	FIXED	IRREGULAR	DISCRETIONARY
Car running costs			
Holiday costs			
Light and heat			
House mortgage			

2   Complete the following sentences:

A **false economy** is

....

....

....

....

A **deficit** is

....

....

....

....

3   What could a family do if they had a deficit in their household budget?

(i)	
(ii)	
(iii)	

4   Name two ways of paying for household groceries other than cash:

(i)	
(ii)	

2 Monday €300 in the kitty Bought milk and bread €4, and biscuits _____ Peter and I each took €5 for lunch	**5 Thursday** Bought milk and bread €4 Peter and I each took €5 for lunch Peter spent €6 on _____
3 Tuesday Bought milk and bread €4, and spent €3 on a _____ Peter and I each took €5 for lunch	**6 Friday** Bought milk and bread €4 Paid €190 for the _____ and another €20 for _____ Lara gave us a loan of _____ Peter and I each took €5 for lunch Peter took _____ for taxi

4 Wednesday Bought milk and bread €4, and chocolates _____ Peter and I each took €5 for lunch	**7 Saturday** Bought milk and bread €4 Took _____ to pay for food for party	**8 Sunday** Bought milk and bread €4

5 Peter and Larry are two students who share a flat. Complete Larry's diary above for last week using information in the conversation below:

Peter: I have no idea where the money is going to.

Larry: Yes, it's only Tuesday and the kitty is nearly empty.

Peter: We put €150 each into that every week.

Larry: I kept a diary of our expenditure last week and I think we need to start budgeting.

Peter: Well, I know we buy bread and milk every day and that's about €4 a week.

Larry: It's €4 a day, Peter! Did you know we spent €5 on biscuits, €3 on a cake and €2 on a box of chocolates last week?

Peter: Ok, but the rent is €190 a week. I know I am correct about that.

Larry: Yes, but we have to pay extra for electricity. Last week that was another €20.

Peter: We also get lunch Monday to Friday in the college. That's €5 each for five days.

Larry: We would have starved last week only Lara gave us a loan of €40. We've got to cut back.

Peter: Well I've been using the bicycle now to go to college. That's a saving.

Larry: Sure, but you spent €15 on a taxi home last Friday. Did you forget the bike?

Peter: I couldn't use the bike and get my suit creased.

Larry: Oh yeah, dry-cleaning the suit was another €6 last Thursday. I hope she was worth it.

Peter: And what about your birthday? That party cost us a fortune.

Larry: €10 for the food is hardly a fortune. Everybody brought their own drink and I was the DJ for the night.

Peter: Do you know you're getting real fussy in your old age!

6 Now complete the following table using information in the conversation:

What is their total income for the week?	
Give an example of fixed expenditure for Peter and Larry.	
Identify an item of irregular expenditure for them.	
Name a discretionary expenditure item they have.	
What is their total expenditure for the week?	
What was their deficit last week?	
How did they finance the deficit?	

7 Choose words from the list below to complete the sentences.

TOTAL   SAVINGS
ESTIMATE   SURPLUS
DISCRETIONARY   BUDGET
INCOME   SALARY
DEFICIT   EXPENDITURE

A .... is a plan which estimates your........................... and expenditure.

Those earning a wage or .... should provide an........................... of their income.

Everyone can help to estimate the .... on fixed, irregular and .... items.

There is a .... if total income is greater than........................... expenditure.

When expenses are greater than income there is a .... in the budget.

To finance this the family could spend less or use their ....

8 Column 1 is a list of words and phrases. Column 2 is a list of descriptions which can be matched to these words and phrases. *(One description cannot be matched.)*

<table>
<tr><td colspan="2">**Column 1**
Words and phrases</td><td colspan="2">**Column 2**
Descriptions</td></tr>
<tr><td>1.</td><td>Current</td><td>A.</td><td>A financial plan</td></tr>
<tr><td>2.</td><td>Loan</td><td>B.</td><td>Doing something cheaply that costs you more than you save</td></tr>
<tr><td>3.</td><td>Durables</td><td>C.</td><td>Regulate</td></tr>
<tr><td>4.</td><td>Budget</td><td>D.</td><td>Borrow money at interest</td></tr>
<tr><td>5.</td><td>Deficit</td><td>E.</td><td>Products that last a long time</td></tr>
<tr><td>6.</td><td>Savings</td><td>F.</td><td>When you have overspent</td></tr>
<tr><td>7.</td><td>Estimate</td><td>G.</td><td>Day-to-day</td></tr>
<tr><td>8.</td><td>Control</td><td>H.</td><td>Money not spent</td></tr>
<tr><td>9.</td><td>False economies</td><td>I.</td><td>Get an approximate idea</td></tr>
<tr><td>10.</td><td>Income</td><td>J.</td><td>Money received</td></tr>
<tr><td></td><td></td><td>K.</td><td>Expenditure</td></tr>
</table>

Match the two lists by placing the letter of the most appropriate description under the relevant number below:

1.	2.	3.	4.	5.	6.	7.	8.	9.	10.

9 Answer true or false to the statements below:
(Tick (✓) the most appropriate box)

	TRUE	FALSE
Car loan repayments are a fixed expense		
Net cash is the difference between total income and expenditure		
An overdraft is a short-term loan		
When there is a surplus this is the amount saved that month		
Child benefit is a source of income for a family		
Going to the cinema is an example of discretionary expenditure		
A mortgage is a loan to buy a house		
The closing cash one month becomes the opening cash the next		

Complete a budget for the Byrne household for the first four months of the year, given the following information.
Opening cash in hand was €90.

Planned income:
- G. Byrne earns €1,950 net per month.
- K. Byrne earns €1,560 net per month.
- Child benefit is €160 per month.

Planned expenditure:
- Annual car tax is €180, due in January.
- House insurance premium amounts to €120 per year, payable in January.
- Annual car insurance of €690 is due for payment in February.
- Car running costs are expected to be €130 per month.
- Household expenses are expected to be €900 per month.
- Electricity bills are expected to be €150 in February and €170 in April.
- Entertainment will cost €160 each month.
- Birthdays will cost €80 in January and €70 in March.

BYRNE HOUSEHOLD	JAN	FEB	MAR	APR	TOTAL
PLANNED INCOME	€	€	€	€	€
G. Byrne – Salary					
K. Byrne – Salary					
Child Benefit					
A. TOTAL INCOME					
PLANNED EXPENDITURE					
Fixed					
Car tax					
House insurance					
Car insurance					
Subtotal					
Irregular					
Car running costs					
Household expenses					
Light and heat					
Subtotal					
Discretionary					
Entertainment costs					
Birthday presents					
Subtotal					
B. TOTAL EXPENDITURE					
Net Cash (A – B)					
Opening Cash					
Closing Cash					

Complete a budget for the McGovern household for June, July, August and September, given the following information.
Opening cash in hand was €360.

Planned income:
- Mr McGovern earns €1,680 net per month.
- Mrs McGovern earns €1,840 net per month.
- Child benefit is €160 per month.

Planned expenditure:
- House mortgage is expected to be €650 per month.
- Annual car insurance €540, due for payment in July.
- Repayments on car loan will cost €160 per month.
- Groceries are usually €700 per month.
- Electricity bills are expected to be €85 in July and €95 in September.
- Car running costs are expected to be €150 per month.
- Birthday presents will be €75 in July.
- Entertainment will cost €80 each month.
- The family expects to spend €1,200 on a holiday in August.

McGOVERN HOUSEHOLD	JUN	JUL	AUG	SEP	TOTAL
PLANNED INCOME	€	€	€	€	€
Mr McGovern – Salary					
Mrs McGovern – Salary					
Child Benefit					
A. TOTAL INCOME					
PLANNED EXPENDITURE					
Fixed					
House mortgage					
Car insurance					
Car loan					
Subtotal					
Irregular					
Groceries					
Light and heat					
Car running costs					
Subtotal					
Discretionary					
Birthday presents					
Entertainment costs					
Holiday					
Subtotal					
B. TOTAL EXPENDITURE					
Net Cash (A – B)					
Opening Cash					
Closing Cash					

Complete a budget for the Egan household for the first four months of the year, given the following information.
Opening cash in hand was €180.

Planned income:
- C. Egan earns €1,250 net per month.
- T. Egan earns €1,460 net per month.
- Child benefit is €160 per month.

Planned expenditure:
- Annual car tax is €140 due in February.
- Repayments on car loan (to be fully paid by the end of March) will cost €200 per month.
- House mortgage is expected to be €460 per month.
- House insurance premium is €120 per year, payable monthly from January.
- Household expenses are expected to be €490 per month.
- Car running costs are expected to be €120 per month, except in February when the annual car service will cost an extra €110.
- Electricity bills are expected to be €90 in February and €80 in April.
- The telephone bill is expected to be €120 in February and €100 in April.
- Birthdays will cost €60 in January and €100 in March.
- Entertainment will cost €120 each month.

EGAN HOUSEHOLD	JAN	FEB	MAR	APR	TOTAL
PLANNED INCOME	€	€	€	€	€
C. Egan – Salary					
T. Egan – Salary					
Child Benefit					
A. TOTAL INCOME					
PLANNED EXPENDITURE					
Fixed					
Car tax					
Car loan					
House mortgage					
House insurance					
Subtotal					
Irregular					
Household expenses					
Car running costs					
Light and heat					
Telephone bills					
Subtotal					
Discretionary					
Birthday presents					
Entertainment costs					
Subtotal					
B. TOTAL EXPENDITURE					
Net Cash (A – B)					
Opening Cash					
Closing Cash					

Complete a budget for the Farrelly household for June, July, August and September, given the following information. Opening cash in hand was €360.

Planned income:
- Mr Farrelly earns €1,760 net per month.
- Mrs Farrelly earns €1,920 net per month.
- Child benefit is €160 per month.

Planned expenditure:
- House mortgage is expected to be €840 per month.
- The house insurance premium of €110 is to be paid in July.
- Annual car insurance €620, due for payment in July.
- Repayments on car loan will cost €240 per month.
- Car running costs are expected to be €210 per month.
- Groceries are usually €900 per month.
- The telephone bill is expected to be €140 in July and €130 in September.
- Electricity bills are expected to be €115 in July and €120 in September.
- A school uniform and books will cost €500 in August.
- Entertainment will cost €200 each month.
- Birthday presents will be €100 in July.
- The family expects to spend €2,300 on a holiday in June.

FARRELLY HOUSEHOLD	JUN	JUL	AUG	SEP	TOTAL
PLANNED INCOME	€	€	€	€	€
Mr Farrelly – Salary					
Mrs Farrelly – Salary					
Child Benefit					
A. TOTAL INCOME					
PLANNED EXPENDITURE					
Fixed					
House mortgage					
House insurance					
Car insurance					
Car loan					
Subtotal					
Irregular					
Car running costs					
Groceries					
Telephone bills					
Light and heat					
School uniform and books					
Subtotal					
Discretionary					
Entertainment costs					
Birthday presents					
Holiday					
Subtotal					
B. TOTAL EXPENDITURE					
Net Cash (A – B)					
Opening Cash					
Closing Cash					

Complete a budget for the Burke household for the first four months of the year, given the following information.
Opening cash in hand was €70.

Planned income:
- P. Burke earns €1,150 net per month.
- M. Burke earns €1,450 net per month.
- Child benefit is €160 per month.

Planned expenditure:
- House insurance premium is €120 per year, payable monthly from January.
- Annual car insurance €400 due for payment in March.
- Annual car tax is €130 due in February.
- Repayments on car loan will cost €300 per month.
- House rental is €800 per month but will increase by €50 from the beginning of March.
- Car running costs are expected to be €110 per month.
- Household expenses are expected to be €800 per month.
- Electricity bills are expected to be €90 in February and €110 in April.
- Entertainment will cost €500 each month.
- Birthdays will cost €90 in January and €80 in March.

BURKE HOUSEHOLD	JAN	FEB	MAR	APR	TOTAL
PLANNED INCOME	€	€	€	€	€
P. Burke – Salary					
M. Burke – Salary					
Child Benefit					
A. TOTAL INCOME					
PLANNED EXPENDITURE					
Fixed					
House insurance					
Car insurance					
Car tax					
Car loan					
House rent					
Subtotal					
Irregular					
Car running costs					
Household expenses					
Light and heat					
Subtotal					
Discretionary					
Entertainment costs					
Birthday presents					
Subtotal					
B. TOTAL EXPENDITURE					
Net Cash (A – B)					
Opening Cash					
Closing Cash					

Complete a budget for the Brady household for June, July, August and September, given the following information. Opening cash in hand was €130.

Planned income:
- Mr Brady earns €1,210 net per month.
- Mrs Brady earns €1,670 net per month.
- Child benefit is €160 per month.

Planned expenditure:
- Annual car insurance €460, due for payment in July.
- Repayments on car loan will cost €350 per month.
- The health insurance premium is €50 per month. This will increase to €60 per month from the beginning of July.
- House mortgage is expected to be €650 per month.
- Electricity bills are expected to be €80 in July and €100 in September.
- Car running costs are expected to be €180 per month.
- Groceries are usually €900 per month.
- The telephone bill is expected to be €120 in July and €140 in September.
- Birthday presents will be €200 in July.
- Entertainment will cost €240 each month.
- The family expects to spend €1,600 on a holiday in July.

BRADY HOUSEHOLD	JUN	JUL	AUG	SEP	TOTAL
PLANNED INCOME	€	€	€	€	€
Mr Brady – Salary					
Mrs Brady – Salary					
Child Benefit					
A. TOTAL INCOME					
PLANNED EXPENDITURE					
Fixed					
Car insurance					
Car loan					
Health insurance					
House mortgage					
Subtotal					
Irregular					
Light and heat					
Car running costs					
Groceries					
Telephone bills					
Subtotal					
Discretionary					
Birthday presents					
Entertainment costs					
Holiday					
Subtotal					
B. TOTAL EXPENDITURE					
Net Cash (A – B)					
Opening Cash					
Closing Cash					

Complete a budget for the Hughes household for the first four months of the year, given the following information.

Opening cash in hand was €150.

Planned income:

- Aidan Hughes earns €1,025 net per month.
- Fiona Hughes earns €850 net per month.
- Child benefit is €160 per month.

Planned expenditure:

- House rental is €600 per month month but will increase by €50 per month from the beginning of March.
- House contents insurance premium of €120 per year is payable monthly from January.
- The Hughes family pays health insurance of €55 per month. This will increase to €60 per month from the beginning of March.
- Groceries are usually €350 per month.
- Aidan pays €50 a month and Fiona pays €55 a month on bus and train fares.
- The family expects to spend €600 on clothes in the January sales.
- Electricity bills are expected to be €95 in January and €80 in March. A fill of heating oil costing €320 will be needed in February.
- A birthday will cost €100 in February.
- Entertainment will cost €120 each month except March, when it will be €300 extra due to a wedding.
- The Hughes family hopes to buy a new television costing €700 in April.

HUGHES HOUSEHOLD	JAN	FEB	MAR	APR	TOTAL
PLANNED INCOME	€	€	€	€	€
Aidan Hughes – Salary					
Fiona Hughes – Salary					
Child Benefit					
A. TOTAL INCOME					
PLANNED EXPENDITURE					
Fixed					
House rental					
Contents insurance					
Health insurance					
Subtotal					
Irregular					
Groceries					
Travel costs					
Clothes					
Light and heat					
Subtotal					
Discretionary					
Birthday					
Entertainment					
TV					
Subtotal					
B. TOTAL EXPENDITURE					
Net Cash (A – B)					
Opening Cash					
Closing Cash					

Complete the budget for the O'Malley family for the year by filling in the figures for the 'Estimates April to December' column and the 'Total for year January to December' column. The following information should be taken into account.

- Enda O'Malley is due a salary increase of five per cent from 1 July.
- Gráinne O'Malley expects to earn an extra €100 per month in November and December.
- Child benefit will increase by €10 per month from 1 October.
- House mortgage is expected to increase by €50 per month from 1 November.
- House insurance, payable monthly, will continue as for the first three months of the year.
- Household costs per month are expected to remain the same for each month until September and to increase by €40 a month beginning in October.
- Car running costs are expected to remain at €60 a month with an additional car service cost of €70 each in June and December.
- Electricity costs for the twelve months (January to December) are estimated at €460.
- The telephone bill is paid every second month and it is estimated that the cost will remain the same as at the beginning of the year.
- Christmas presents are expected to cost €230 in December.
- Entertainment is estimated at €750 for the twelve months (January to December).
- The family holiday in August is expected to cost €1,000.

O'MALLEY HOUSEHOLD	JAN	FEB	MAR	Total Jan–Mar	Estimates Apr–Dec	Total for year Jan–Dec
PLANNED INCOME	€	€	€	€	€	€
Enda O'Malley – Salary	560	560	560	1,680		
Gráinne O'Malley – Salary	580	580	580	1,740		
Child Benefit	40	40	40	120		
A. TOTAL INCOME	1,180	1,180	1,180	3,540		
PLANNED EXPENDITURE						
Fixed						
House mortgage	320	320	320	960		
Car insurance	270			270		
Annual car tax	180			180		
House insurance	15	15	15	45		
Subtotal	785	335	335	1,455		
Irregular						
Household costs	480	480	480	1,440		
Car running costs	60	60	60	180		
Light and heat		75		75		
Telephone	90		90	180		
Subtotal	630	615	630	1,875		
Discretionary						
Presents			40	40		
Entertainment	40	55	35	130		
Holidays						
Subtotal	40	55	75	170		
B. TOTAL EXPENDITURE	1,455	1,005	1,040	3,500		
Net Cash (A – B)	(275)	175	140	40		
Opening Cash	100	(175)	0	100		
Closing Cash	(175)	0	140	140		

Chapter 4

Being a good *consumer*

1 Find the following words hidden in this grid, as in the example:

Goods ✓

Service

Consumer

False

Economies

Ingredients

Price

Receipt

Guarantee

Deposit

G	O	F	D	S	P	S	R	E	I	C
R	C	O	A	R	U	M	V	R	N	D
G	E	R	I	L	C	E	I	P	G	T
U	S	C	O	N	S	U	M	E	R	A
A	E	D	E	V	O	E	S	P	E	D
R	R	P	R	I	O	G	O	O	D	S
A	V	S	A	N	P	U	R	T	I	P
N	I	M	I	E	S	T	V	R	E	C
T	C	G	R	S	D	S	I	E	N	T
E	E	O	D	E	P	O	S	I	T	E
E	E	C	O	N	O	M	I	E	S	R

2 Tick (✓) whether each of the following are goods or services:

	GOODS	SERVICES
Buying a ticket for the cinema		
Buying sweets		
Buying a train ticket		
Buying a magazine		
Buying a computer game		

3 List **four** items written on a receipt:

(i)
....

(ii)
....

(iii)
....

(iv)
....

4 In each space below, write the most appropriate word or term from the following list:

DEPOSIT   INGREDIENTS   CREDIT CARD   RECEIPT   BAR CODE   CREDIT NOTE
(One of the words/terms above does not complete any of the sentences below.)

(i) The .... is a series of vertical lines representing numbers.

(ii) The .... are given in descending order of weight.

(iii) A .... is a small part of the overall cost of the goods.

(iv) A .... entitles you to buy something else in the shop.

(v) The document which provides proof of payment is called a ....

5 Explain the term **False Economy**:

....

....

....

6 Find a word in the list to complete the words in the table:

credit

bar

unit

false

....	code
....	economy
....	note
....	price

7 Column 1 is a list of words and phrases. Column 2 is a list of descriptions which can be matched to these words and phrases. *(One description cannot be matched.)*

Column 1	Column 2
Words and phrases	**Descriptions**

Column 1 — Words and phrases:
1. Ingredients
2. Goods
3. Consumer
4. Guarantee
5. Origin
6. Credit note
7. Unit price
8. Advertisement
9. Bar code
10. Receipt

Column 2 — Descriptions:
A. Anyone who uses goods or services
B. A series of vertical lines on a product label
C. The price divided by the quantity
D. The sources of goods
E. This entitles you to buy something else in the shop
F. The components of a product
G. The way goods are promoted
H. Proof of purchase
I. The money refunded
J. Products
K. This usually lasts a year

Match the two lists by placing the letter of the most appropriate description under the relevant number below:

1.	2.	3.	4.	5.	6.	7.	8.	9.	10.

8 Tick (✓) whether each of the following is true or false:

	TRUE	FALSE
A shop must return your deposit if you change your mind about wanting the product.		
Never send cash in the post.		
A receipt shows evidence of purchase.		
A shop can insist that you accept a credit note.		
A 100g jar of coffee for €4.00 is better money value than a 200g jar of coffee for €5.50.		

9 List **five** items of information found on the label of a food product:

(i)
....

(ii)
....

(iii)
....

(iv)
....

(v)
....

10 A consumer is defined as:

A person who manages a business ☐

A person who contacts clients by e-mail ☐

A person who buys goods for private use ☐

(Tick (✓) the most appropriate box)

eTest.ie
Try a test on this topic

11 List **three** questions you should ask yourself before buying anything:

(i)
....

(ii)
....

(iii)
....

12 Calculate the unit price for each of the following boxes of cereal:

SIZE	PRICE	WEIGHT	UNIT PRICE
SMALL	€1.58	400 g	
MEDIUM	€2.70	750 g	
LARGE	€3.90	1 kg	

Open for Business **Workbook**

Chapter 5
Consumer *rights*

1 Name the law that protects the rights of consumers.

....

....

2 In each space below, write the most appropriate word or term from the following list:

> CONFORM   PURPOSE   MERCHANTABLE   DESCRIBED   GUARANTEE
> *(One of the words above does not complete any of the sentences below.)*

   (i)   Goods should be of .... quality.

   (ii)   Goods should be fit for their ....

   (iii)   Goods should be as ....

   (iv)   Goods should .... to sample.

3 Are you entitled to a complete refund in each of these cases? Tick (✓) the correct box.

	TRUE	FALSE
The salesperson in a shop insists a new game will work on your computer. You buy the game but it does not work.		
You buy a pair of shoes. They break within a week but you continue to wear them and do not complain until six months later.		
You go to the cinema but half-way through the film you realise it is stupid and you should have gone to a different movie.		
You buy a bar of chocolate and when you unwrap it you see that it is bad.		
You buy a watch and the strap breaks within a week. You immediately return to the shop.		

4 Explain the term **Caveat Emptor**:

....

....

....

....

5 What steps should be taken when making a complaint?

(i)
....

(ii)
....

(iii)
....

(iv)
....

6 Column 1 is a list of words and phrases. Column 2 is a list of descriptions which can be matched to these words and phrases. *(One description cannot be matched.)*

Column 1 **Words and phrases**	Column 2 **Descriptions**
1. Guarantee	A. To make it known that something is wrong
2. Refund	B. Getting a new product for an old one
3. Retailer	C. A piece of law
4. Replacement	D. Some form of compensation
5. Repair	E. Someone who sells goods and services
6. Act	F. A promise that ensures the product should be perfect when sold
7. Complain	G. Fixing a fault in a product
8. Remedy	H. When the product is not fully correct
9. Misuse	I. The money returned if something is wrong with the product
10. Receipt	J. To treat a product in the wrong way
	K. A document given to prove you bought something

Match the two lists by placing the letter of the most appropriate description under the relevant number below:

1.	2.	3.	4.	5.	6.	7.	8.	9.	10.

7 Read the following email:

From:	carol@freemail.com
To:	john@computercity.net
Subject:	Agreement at last

Dear Mr Molloy

I am glad we were finally able to reach an agreement today, 8 August. It is four months since I made my initial complaint on 4 April, when I told you about the problem I was having with the computer I bought on 29 February.

On 11 July you offered to replace it. I was not happy with this. I stopped using the computer on 7 March but it was not until 9 May that you offered to repair it, but I wanted to get a complete refund. When I brought it back to you on 6 June you said there was nothing you could do for me.

Yours truly

Carol

What happened on each of these dates mentioned in the email above?

(a) 29 February

....

(b) 7 March

....

(c) 4 April

....

(d) 9 May

....

(e) 6 June

....

(f) 11 July

....

(g) 8 August

....

8 Peter and Lisa Moore live at 18 Lake View, Atlantic Drive, Co. Donegal. They booked a family holiday costing €2,600 with Sunnyside Travel Ltd, Letterkenny, Co. Donegal for two weeks in Portugal from 1 June to 15 June. The holiday brochure clearly stated that the beach was five minutes' walk from their apartment. On arrival at their apartment, the Moores discovered that the closest beach was five kilometres away. They were very disappointed.

On 16 June, after they returned home, Lisa Moore wrote a letter of complaint to the manager of Sunnyside Travel Ltd requesting suitable redress.

Write the letter below that Lisa sent to Sunnyside Travel Ltd.

1 Match the products on the left with the claims on the right, as in the example.

PRODUCTS		CLAIMS	
1.	Jam	A.	PC compatible
2.	Chair	B.	Will not shrink
3.	Radiator	C.	Childproof
4.	Builder	D.	Genuine silk
5.	Taxi service	E.	Satellite channels in all rooms
6.	Supermarket	F.	Stainless steel
7.	Disco	G.	Solid gold
8.	Computer game	H.	Fireproof
9.	Jumper	I.	Solid oak
10.	Knife	J.	Luxury drive
11.	Hotel	K.	Home-made
12.	Car door	L.	Well stocked
13.	Tie	M.	No job too small
14.	Wedding ring	N.	Dancing until 2 a.m.
15.	Suite of furniture	O.	Will not leak

2 Under Irish consumer law, are shops allowed to display the following notices?
(Tick (✓) either YES or NO in each case.)

We do not accept credit cards	
YES	NO

Goods will not be exchanged	
YES	NO

3 Tick (✓) whether each of the following is true or false:

	TRUE	FALSE
A sweater is priced at €19 in the shop window and €27 inside the shop. You have the right to insist on the sweater for €19.		
You buy a pair of trainers and one year later the sole breaks. You have the right to insist on a complete refund from the shop.		
You buy a school bag that the shop manager says is pure leather. A week later you discover a label inside the bag that states the bag is plastic. You have the right to insist on a complete refund.		
You see a washing machine in a shop marked €560, with a label 'free delivery to all areas'. The shop assistant asks you to pay an extra €40 delivery charge because you live too far away. You have the right to insist on the free delivery.		
You go into the Galway branch of a nationwide chain of stores to buy a coat advertised on television for €75. However, the coat is marked as €90. The assistant says the €75 price applies to the Cork branch only. You have the right to insist on the coat for €75.		

4 Name the law that protects consumers from false and misleading advertisements.

....

....

5 Explain the term **Third Party**:

....

....

....

6 Who publishes *Consumer Choice* magazine?

....

....

7 Column 1 is a list of words and phrases. Column 2 is a list of descriptions which can be matched to these words and phrases. *(One description cannot be matched.)*

Column 1 **Words and phrases**	Column 2 **Descriptions**
1. Consumer	A. A slogan about a product or service
2. Offence	B. A person who uses goods and services
3. Ombudsman	C. Something that fixes a complaint
4. Claim	D. Making up for damage done
5. Trader	E. Not telling the full truth
6. Remedy	F. Something that is legally wrong
7. Mislead	G. When the price of a product rises suddenly
8. Compensation	H. Before now
9. Previous	I. Suggested
10. Recommended	J. Investigates complaints against companies
	K. A person who buys and sells to consumers

Match the two lists by placing the letter of the most appropriate description under the relevant number below:

1.	2.	3.	4.	5.	6.	7.	8.	9.	10.

8 In each space below, write the most appropriate word or term from the following list:

CONSUMER   TRADE   INFORMATION   CLAIMS   OMBUDSMAN   ASSOCIATION
(One of the words/terms above does not complete any of the sentences below.)

(i)   The small .... court costs very little.

(ii)   RGDATA is an example of a .... association.

(iii)   If you have a complaint against An Post you could complain to the ....

(iv)   The Director of .... Affairs publishes pamphlets to inform consumers.

(v)   The Consumer .... Act protects consumers from false advertisements.

9 Lisa Walsh (lisa@freemail.com) bought a GHD on 20 March from Online Electrics (elec@gmail.com).

After using it for a week, the on/off switch stopped working.

She posted the item back to Online Electrics and sent them an email asking them for a replacement.

Write the email Lisa sent to Online Electrics.

From:	lisa@freemail.com
To:	
Subject:	

Chapter 7
Money and *banking*

1 Find the following words hidden in this grid:

Barter ✓

Cheque

DIRT

Save

Payee

Drawee

Drawer

Endorse

Cross

Blank

B	U	C	H	E	Q	U	E	A	D	R
A	E	Q	R	P	E	Y	S	V	S	E
V	E	D	E	O	O	W	E	N	D	A
R	A	B	S	H	R	S	A	V	E	O
E	B	L	A	P	C	D	E	R	N	S
E	O	A	E	H	T	R	C	E	D	S
Y	R	N	R	D	I	A	O	R	O	O
V	S	K	O	T	Y	W	C	S	R	D
A	E	P	A	Y	E	E	A	P	S	N
S	S	R	I	D	I	R	T	O	E	E

2 What do the following letters stand for? *(Write **each** answer in full in the space provided.)*

ATM	
PIN	
DIRT	

3 In each space below, write the most appropriate word from the following list:

> MORTGAGE   CURRENT   DIRT   CREDIT   COMMERCIAL   BONDS
> *(One of the words/terms above does not complete any of the sentences below.)*

(i) Savers in a _____ union get interest in the form of a dividend each year.

(ii) AIB is an example of a _____ bank.

(iii) Holders of _____ accounts get a cheque book.

(iv) You can buy savings _____ in the Post Office.

(v) A _____ loan is used to buy a house.

4 Tick (✓) whether each of the following is true or false:

	TRUE	FALSE
Crossing a cheque makes it safer.		
Legal tender is the official currency of a country.		
A seven-month-old cheque can still be cashed.		
If you sign the back of a cheque you can pass the cheque on to someone else as payment of a debt.		
Money is anything which is acceptable by people in exchange for goods and services.		

5 Complete this table below using the words and terms in the list:

Legal tender	_____	Debit card
Laser card	_____	Notes and coins
Credit card	_____	American Express
Charge card	_____	Swapping goods
Barter	_____	Visa

6 Aisling Murphy, who will be 24 years of age on 21 August, lives at 14 Emmet Street, Clonmel, Co. Tipperary (her native county). Her home telephone number is 052 654987 and her mobile phone number is 086 123654. Her email address is aislingmurphy@bloflo.ie. She is not married.

Two weeks ago Aisling commenced full-time employment as a florist with Blooms Florist Ltd, 38 Mitchel Street, Clonmel, Co. Tipperary. Her gross salary is €24,000 per year, payable monthly. As her new employer wants to pay her salary by Paypath, she has decided to open a current account. Today, she calls into the local branch of Bank of Ireland. Complete the application form below:

Bank of Ireland
CURRENT ACCOUNT APPLICATION FORM

PERSONAL DETAILS

Surname .... Mr, Mrs, Ms ....

First Name .... Male/Female ....

Home Address ....

....

Date of Birth ....

Country of Birth .... Married/Single ....

EMPLOYMENT DETAILS

Occupation ....

Employer ....

Gross salary per month ....

Length of time in your present employment ....

Will your income be paid into your bank account? Yes/No ....

CONTACT DETAILS

Home Telephone Number ....

Mobile Telephone Number ....

Email Address ....

Please open a current account in my name.

I certify the accuracy of the information given above.

SIGNATURE .... DATE ....

7 Use the words in the list below to name the parts of the cheque:

Counterfoil	Cheque number	Date
Stamp	Drawee	Bank sort code
Amount in words	Amount in figures	Drawer
Payee	Current account number	

(a) ....

(b) ....

(d) ....

(c) ....

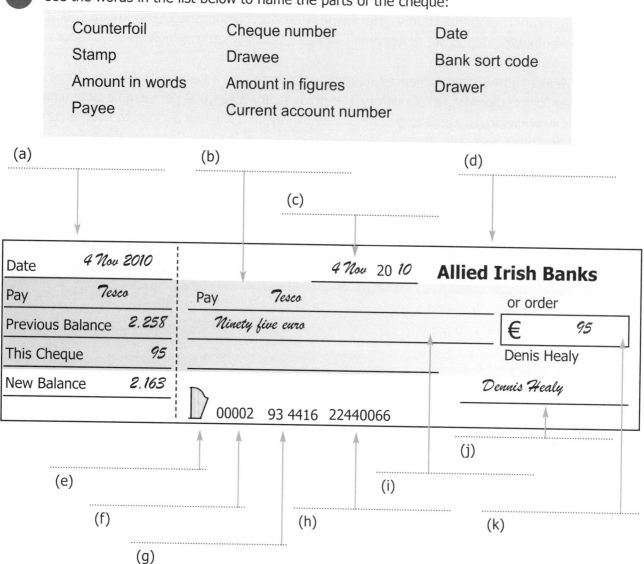

(e) ....

(f) ....

(g) ....

(h) ....

(i) ....

(j) ....

(k) ....

8 On 15 April, Harry O'Dwyer went into Gofar Travel Ltd to book a holiday. He paid a deposit of €500 by cheque, crossing it to make it as safe as possible.

Complete the cheque and counterfoil:

Date		20	**Allied Irish Banks**
Pay	Pay		or order
Previous Balance 950			€
This Cheque			Harry O'Dwyer
New Balance	00268 53 2638 52588539		

9 Complete fully the following cheque using the information provided.

Date	14 Dec 2010				20	**Allied Irish Banks**
Pay	Tina Gaffney	Pay				or order
Previous Balance	830					€
This Cheque	120					Mark O'Connor
New Balance	710					

00125   94 5427   44221155

10 Look at the cheque above and complete the following:

(i) Name the drawer of the cheque: ....

(ii) Name the drawee of the cheque: ....

(iii) Name the payee of the cheque: ....

11 Complete fully the following cheque using the information provided.

Date	17 Jan 2010				20	**Bank of Ireland**
Pay	Thomas Keogh	Pay				or order
Previous Balance	640					€
This Cheque	190					Joanna Bulger
New Balance	450					

00078   84 2218   55881133

12 Look at the cheque above and complete the following:

(i) Name the drawer of the cheque: ....

(ii) Name the drawee of the cheque: ....

(iii) Name the payee of the cheque: ....

Helen O'Flanagan receives the following bank statement:

Bank Statement				
Date	Particulars	Debit	Credit	Balance
May		€	€	€
1	Balance forward			1,500
2	Paypath		640	2,140
4	Cheque no. 1	53		2,087
5	ATM Mullingar	200		1,887
6	Cheque no. 5	34		1,853
7	Paypath		640	2,493
8	Cheque no. 4	42		2,451
11	Standing order	1,000		1,451
12	Bank charges	15		1,436

13 Is this a deposit account or a current account? Give a reason for your answer.

....

....

....

14 Why are the cheque numbers not in sequence?

....

....

....

15 Explain the transaction on May 5.

....

....

....

16 Explain how a **Standing Order** works.

....

....

....

The following is Helen's own record of her bank transactions.

Dr					Bank Account			Cr
Date	Details	F	Total	Date	Details	F	Total	
May			€	May			€	
1	Balance	b/d	1,500	3	Petrol	1	53	
2	Wages		640	4	Car service	2	120	
7	Lottery win		500	5	Groceries	ATM	200	
				5	Electric World	3	900	
				5	Groceries	4	42	
				6	Cinema	5	34	
				7	Balance	c/d	1,291	
			2,640				2,640	
8	Balance	b/d	1,291					

17 Make whatever adjustments are necessary to bring her records up to date.

Dr				Bank Account			Cr
Date	Details	F	Total	Date	Details	F	Total
			€				€

18 Prepare a bank reconciliation statement for Helen.

Bank Reconciliation Statement					
			€	€	€

19 Explain the term **Bounced Cheque**:

....

....

....

20 Tick (✓) whether each of the following are income or expenditure:

	INCOME	EXPENDITURE
Mr Malone received his wages		
Paid for petrol by cheque		
Withdrew cash from ATM to pay for groceries		
Mr Malone sold his car and received €4,000		
Paid mortgage by standing order		

21 Column 1 is a list of words and phrases. Column 2 is a list of descriptions which can be matched to these words and phrases. *(One description cannot be matched.)*

Column 1 Words and phrases	Column 2 Descriptions
1. DIRT	A. Sign the back of a cheque
2. Save	B. Swapping goods and services
3. Endorse	C. The person writing the cheque
4. Crossing	D. Money you don't spend until later
5. Statement	E. The person receiving the cheque
6. Drawer	F. The currency in daily use
7. ATM	G. A letter sent by the bank to the customer
8. Legal tender	H. A tax on savings
9. Payee	I. The bank that issues the cheque book
10. Barter	J. Cash dispenser
	K. Making a cheque safer

eTest.ie
Try a test on this topic

Match the two lists by placing the letter of the most appropriate description under the relevant number below:

1.	2.	3.	4.	5.	6.	7.	8.	9.	10.

Chapter 8

Borrowing *money*

① Name **two** laws that protect the rights of borrowers.

(i) ....

(ii) ....

② In each space below, write the most appropriate word from the following list:

PURCHASE   MORTGAGE   OVERDRAFT   CREDIT   MEDIUM   CURRENT
(One of the words above does not complete any of the sentences below.)

(i) .... cards can be used for short-term borrowing.

(ii) A bank .... is available to people with a .... account.

(iii) Hire .... can be used to buy a car.

(iv) A .... is a long-term loan used to buy a house.

③ Tick (✓) the box to indicate the most appropriate source of finance from the options given.

	CREDIT UNION	CREDIT CARD	MORTGAGE	HP
A teenager wishes to buy a bicycle. She can pay €5 each week off a loan.				
An engaged couple wants to buy a house.				
A woman needs to purchase a car. She can afford to pay out €100 each month, and she doesn't live near any credit union.				
A family wishes to borrow €1,800 for a holiday.				
A man is temporarily short of money and is in a shop planning to buy a DVD player.				

4 What do the following letters stand for? (Write **each** answer in full in the space provided.)

HP	
APR	
CAR	

5 When will a loan normally be granted? (Give four reasons.)

(i) ....

(ii) ....

(iii) ....

(iv) ....

6 Column 1 is a list of words and phrases. Column 2 is a list of descriptions which can be matched to these words and phrases. *(One description cannot be matched.)*

Column 1	Column 2
Words and phrases	**Descriptions**
1. Guarantor	A. Buying something and paying for it later
2. Collateral	B. A long-term loan
3. Credit	C. Security for a loan
4. Overdraft	D. Each year
5. Mortgage	E. The real cost of a loan
6. Interest	F. An agreement between people
7. Per annum	G. The price of credit
8. Bankrupt	H. Someone who pays your debt if you cannot
9. APR	I. The amount of the repayment each month
10. Instalment	J. Not able to pay your debts
	K. A short-term loan

Match the two lists by placing the letter of the most appropriate description under the relevant number below:

1.	2.	3.	4.	5.	6.	7.	8.	9.	10.

Read the following and answer the questions below.

Ross has no cash left after too many party nights and it will be another two days before he gets his wages. In the meantime he needs €80 to buy some groceries in the local supermarket.

Carol has plenty of expensive jewellery but no cash and she needs to borrow €700 to go on holiday. She will repay the loan over the next twelve months.

George has an expensive boat but he wants to buy a car. He has no money so he needs a loan of €11,000. He will take three years to repay this loan.

Rachel is making the biggest purchase of her life: she wants to buy an apartment. She does not have enough money so she needs a loan of €180,000 for the next twenty years.

7 The following figures are mentioned. What do they relate to?

(a) €80 ....

(b) €700 ....

(c) €11,000 ....

(d) €180,000 ....

(e) Two days ....

(f) Twelve months ....

(g) Twenty years ....

8 Read the information about Ross.

(a) How long does he need a loan for? ....

(b) Why would a credit card be a suitable source of finance for him? ....

....

(c) Name another source of finance that he could use. ....

(d) Why wouldn't it be a good idea for him to use a medium-term loan? ....

....

9 Complete this table.

	TERM OF LOAN	TYPE OF LOAN	COLLATERAL
Ross			
Carol			
George			
Rachel			

10 Monica Ryan, who is single, lives at 45 Chapel Road, Cork, in a house which she purchased in 2000 with the help of a mortgage of €200,000 from the Educational Building Society and to whom she repays €1,200 per month. Her telephone number is 021 654987.

Monica is employed as a theatre nurse in the Cork University Hospital, where she started work in 1990. She earns a gross salary of €3,000 per month, out of which she pays income tax and PRSI totalling €870 per month.

Monica wishes to buy a car for her next birthday. She was 35 years old last 8 July. In order to buy the car, she needs to borrow €15,000 which she hopes to repay in monthly instalments of €450 over the next three years. She is already paying the Cork Credit Union €150 per month for a loan of €5,000 which she obtained two years ago.

Complete the application form below:

Allied Irish Banks
LOAN APPLICATION FORM

PERSONAL DETAILS

Name	Mr, Mrs, Ms ....
Address	
Number of years at this address	Owner or rented ....
Date of birth	
Telephone	
Mortgage amount	
Annual repayments on mortgage	
Mortgage borrowed from	

EMPLOYMENT DETAILS

Occupation ....
Employer's address ....
Net salary per month ....
Length of time in your present employment ....

LOAN REQUIRED

Amount ....
Purpose ....
How long do you want the loan for? ....
How much can you repay each month? ....

DETAILS OF OTHER EXISTING LOANS

Lender	Amount	Annual repayments
....		

SIGNATURE .... DATE ....

Chapter 9
Personal *insurance*

1 Find the following words hidden in this grid, as in the example:

Risks ✓

Insurable

Broker

Endowment

Assess

Utmost

Discount

Surrender

Encash

Actuary

```
R E U T M O S T U A S H
E I S Y O B U S N S E S
I N S U R A B L E S N T
H S D O U A S N T S D E
S U K O N C C T D E S S
B E E C W A U T M O K A
R Y R A S M R E U R S N
O S U H T R E N D A I D
S D S U R R E N D E R E
T D I S C O U N T U M Y
R A S H E N C T R A S H
```

2 Explain the term **Non-insurable Risks**:

....

....

....

3 Tick (✓) whether each of the following is true or false:

	TRUE	FALSE
You can insure yourself against the risk of failing your Junior Cert.		
A husband may insure his wife's life and she may insure his life.		
A loading reduces the premium you pay.		
All cars must have fully comprehensive insurance.		
Fully comprehensive insurance is usually more expensive than third, party, fire and theft.		

4 List **four** principles of insurance.

(i)
....

(ii)
....

(iii)
....

(iv)
....

5 A house has a market value of €400,000 but is only insured for €300,000. If a carpet valued at €1,000 is damaged, how much compensation will be paid?

ANSWER	WORKINGS

6 Explain the term **No-claims Bonus**:

....

....

....

7 Column 1 is a list of words and phrases. Column 2 is a list of descriptions which can be matched to these words and phrases. *(One description cannot be matched.)*

Column 1	Column 2
Words and phrases	**Descriptions**

1. Actuary	A. Money paid to an insurance company
2. Assessor	B. When the insurance company takes over your rights
3. Premium	C. To stop the policy
4. Proposal form	D. Calculates the amount of the insurance premium
5. Subrogation	E. The contract prepared by the insurance company
6. Utmost good faith	F. An extra premium charge
7. Policy	G. Recommends the amount of compensation
8. Cover note	H. The commission charged by a broker
9. Encash	I. Must answer all questions truthfully
10. Brokerage	J. A temporary insurance
	K. Application form for insurance

Match the two lists by placing the letter of the most appropriate description under the relevant number below:

1.	2.	3.	4.	5.	6.	7.	8.	9.	10.

8 In each space below, write the most appropriate word from the following list:

FIRE   INTEREST   DISCOUNT   ADJUSTER   ASSURANCE   GOOD
(One of the words above does not complete any of the sentences below.)

(i) Risks that will happen are covered under life .... policies.

(ii) There may be a .... if the house has an alarm.

(iii) Third party, ... and theft.

(iv) The loss .... is hired by the insurance company.

(v) Utmost .... faith.

9 Sasha Brady, a bank official, who lives at 76 Seaview Avenue, Rosses Point, Sligo, wishes to insure her house and its contents for one year for €370,000. It is a detached concrete house in an area which was never flooded and it has never been damaged in any way since it was built.

Sasha and her family were never in any trouble with the law. She never had any problem getting insurance in the past. The only valuable articles she has in the house are jewellery valued at €3,500, a computer valued at €1,100 and furniture and clothing valued at €6,000.

Complete Sasha's proposal form using today's date.

AIB Home Insurance
PROPOSAL FORM

PERSONAL DETAILS

Name .... Mr, Mrs, Ms ....

Address ....

....

Occupation ....

Insurance required from: .... To: ....

HOUSE DETAILS

Tick (✓) Yes or No in answer to each of the following: Yes   No

1. Is your house: (i)   built of stone/concrete?   ☐   ☐

                           (ii) subject to flooding?   ☐   ☐

                           (iii) detached?   ☐   ☐

2. Has your house been previously damaged?   ☐   ☐

3. Have you or your family (i)   been convicted of any crime?   ☐   ☐

                            (ii) ever been refused insurance?   ☐   ☐

4. State how much cover you require: ....

5. Apart from furniture and clothing, name any articles valued over €1,000:

....

....

SIGNATURE ....   DATE ....

Chapter 10

What is *economics?*

1 Match the factors of production on the left with the rewards on the right, as in the example.

FACTORS OF PRODUCTION

1. Land
2. Labour
3. Capital (Savings)
4. Enterprise

REWARDS

A. Interest
B. Profit
C. Wages
D. Rent

2 Tick (✓) the factor of production which applies to each item listed below.

	LAND	LABOUR	CAPITAL	ENTERPRISE
Managers				
Oil				
Shareholders				
Equipment				

3 Circle Ireland's economic resources from the items listed below, as in the example.

Diamonds

Bank deposits

Fertile land

Coffee

Wood

Natural gas

Oranges

Tobacco

Wool

Wheat

Rubber

Live animals

Cocoa

Fish

4 Tick (✓) whether each of the following is true or false:

	TRUE	FALSE
There are four factors of production.		
Inflation is bad for savers.		
Wage increases can cause inflation.		
When interest rates are high loans are expensive and people won't borrow as much.		
During a recession there is an increase in the number of people employed.		

5 Explain the term **Inflation**:

....

....

....

6 Fill in the two missing factors of production in the spaces provided.

LAND		CAPITAL	

7 Amy's teacher asks her to summarise this chapter for her homework. Complete her homework using words from the following list:

> INFLATION   CONSUMERS   LABOUR   ENTERPRISE   NEGATIVE
> RATES   CAPITAL   SERVICES   ECONOMY   BUSINESS
> *(One of the words above does not complete any of the sentences below.)*

An .... is a system which provides goods and...

for .... The performance of the economy has a positive or

.... effect on .... Since an economy is dependent

on land, ... , capital and .... , many things can affect its

performance, such as unemployment, interest .... and ....

8 Column 1 is a list of words and phrases. Column 2 is a list of descriptions which can be matched to these words and phrases. *(One description cannot be matched.)*

Column 1 **Words and phrases**	Column 2 **Descriptions**
1. Scarcity	A. Things used to create wealth
2. Inflation	B. This is paid to people for the use of their land
3. Resources	C. A risk taker
4. Labour	D. When production decreases
5. Rent	E. Rising prices
6. Capital	F. Selecting between actions
7. Entrepreneur	G. The official measure of economic growth
8. CPI	H. When there is not enough of something
9. GNP	I. The money needed to run a business
10. Recession	J. The official measure of inflation in Ireland
	K. The human resources needed to make something

Match the two lists by placing the letter of the most appropriate description under the relevant number below:

1.	2.	3.	4.	5.	6.	7.	8.	9.	10.

9 Explain the term **Recession**:

....

....

....

10 What do the following letters stand for? *(Write **each** answer in full in the space provided.)*

CPI	
GNP	

11 Fill in the two missing factors of production in the spaces provided.

	LABOUR		**ENTERPRISE**

12 Draw a line graph or bar chart to show the following rates of inflation in a country:

Year:	2006	2007	2008	2009	2010
Rate:	7%	3%	5%	6%	2%

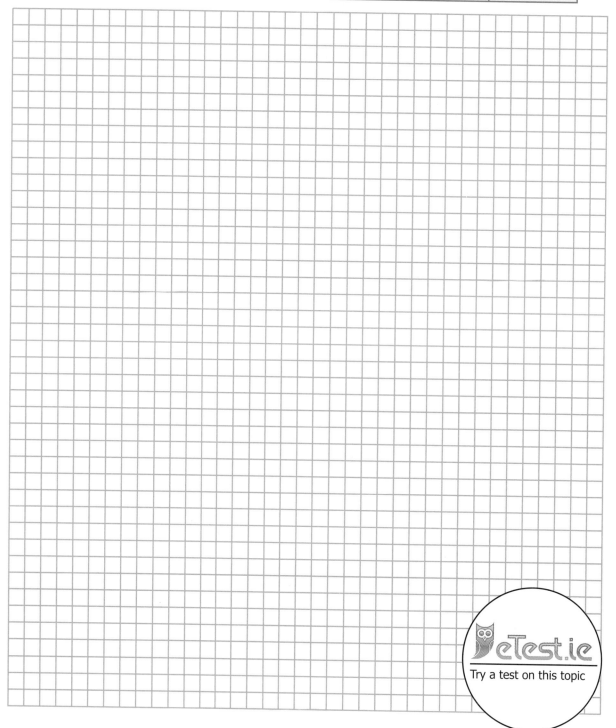

1 In which month does Budget Day usually occur?

....

2 Which government department prepares the national budget?

....

3 What do the following letters stand for? *(Write **each** answer in full in the space provided.)*

VAT	
DIRT	

4 Tick (✓) the box to show whether these are examples of capital or current expenditure.

	Capital expenditure	Current expenditure
Paying nurses' salaries.		
Social welfare payments.		
Development of new airport terminal.		
Purchase of new army rifles.		
Purchase of bullets for army rifles.		
Building a new tunnel under the River Lee.		
Building extension to community school.		
Paying teachers' salaries.		
Construction of new tourist interpretative centre.		
Construction of new prison.		

5 Tick (✓) the box to indicate the most appropriate effect on the national budget.

	More expenditure on pensions	Less expenditure on pensions	More expenditure on education	Less expenditure on education
Government decides to reduce the number of students in each class.				
Government decides to shorten the school day.				
Government decides that children should not be allowed to begin school until they are seven years of age.				
New medical advances cause people to live longer.				
New unknown disease kills thousands of people over sixty years of age.				
Government decides to allow people to retire at fifty-five rather than sixty-five.				

To: Roinn An Taoisigh
From: An Roinn Airgeadais
RE: Budget Day

Taoiseach, a Chara

I have received all the estimates from the various departments and interested bodies. In advance of Budget Day I would like to inform you that some difficult decisions will have to be made in regard to government spending over the coming year. I would like to put forward the following proposals.

(1) Most grants for new school buildings and repairs will have to be cancelled for this year.
(2) I propose to increase the pension age from sixty-five to seventy years of age.
(3) Present work on monuments and parks will cease immediately.
(4) I propose to increase the excise duty on cigarettes by eighty cent.
(5) I propose to put a forty cent tax on chewing gum. This should reduce the demand for chewing gum and help make our streets cleaner.
(6) We could also consider selling off the ESB.

I look forward to your support in these proposals on Budget Day.

Mise le Meas
Minister for Finance

6 Study the fax from the Minister for Finance to the Taoiseach and answer these questions.

(a) What capital expenditure does the minister wish to cancel?

....

(b) Are repairs to school buildings an example of capital or current expenditure?

....

(c) What effect will increasing the pension age have on the budget?

....

(d) What effect will a forty cent tax on chewing gum have?

....

(e) Which state company does the minister wish to privatise?

....

(f) Which expressions in the fax mean the following?

(i) The time you can retire. ....

(ii) The tax on tobacco. ....

(iii) Privatising. ....

(iv) Non-repayable source of money. ....

(v) Lower the number buying. ....

7 List **three** options open to the government when they have a budget surplus:

(i)
....

(ii)
....

(iii)
....

8 Explain the difference between **Capital** and **Current Expenditure**:

....

....

....

....

9 (a) Draft a national budget from the following information:

Main items of Revenue and Expenditure	€ Millions
Debt Servicing	190
PAYE	2,550
VAT	1,470
Health Services	1,720
Social Welfare	1,230
Education and Science	1,340
Corporation Tax	260
Customs Duties	235

National Budget			
	Current Income			€ million
	Total Income			
	Current Expenditure			
	Total Expenditure			
	Difference			

(b) Estimate and identify whether there is a deficit or a surplus.

....

....

....

....

eTest.ie
Try a test on this topic

Chapter 12
Foreign *trade*

1 Circle the EU member states from the countries listed below, as in the example.

Australia	Latvia
(Austria)	Lithuania
Belgium	Luxembourg
Bulgaria	Malta
China	Netherlands
Cyprus	New Zealand
Czech Republic	Norway
Denmark	Poland
Estonia	Portugal
Finland	Romania
France	Russia
Germany	Slovakia
Greece	Slovenia
Hungary	Spain
Iceland	Sweden
India	Switzerland
Ireland	United Kingdom
Italy	USA
Japan	

2 Explain the term **Foreign Trade**:

....

....

....

3 Name one difficulty of exporting.

....

4 List **three** Irish imports and **three** Irish exports.

IMPORTS

(i) ....

(ii) ....

(iii) ....

EXPORTS

(i) ....

(ii) ....

(iii) ....

5 Tick (✓) which category each of the following belongs to:

	Visible import	Visible export	Invisible import	Invisible export
Irish horses winning prize money in England.				
Italian shoes bought in Ireland.				
Irish people holidaying in Spain.				
American people hiring Irish aircraft.				
Irish cheese sold to a French customer.				
Irish family buys subscription to Sky Sports.				
Aer Lingus ticket bought by a German tourist.				
Spanish oranges bought in Ireland.				
Dutch family rents a holiday cottage in Clare.				
Japanese cars bought in Ireland.				

6 Name the currency which is **legal tender** in each country below.

COUNTRY	CURRENCY
France	
USA	
United Kingdom	
Spain	

Bureau de Change			
COUNTRY	CURRENCY	BANK SELLS	BANK BUYS
Britain	Pound (£)	0.68	0.72
Norway	Krone (Kr)	7.27	7.70
USA	Dollar ($)	1.11	1.16
Japan	Yen (¥)	1.32	1.41

7 Using the rates above, answer the following.

ANSWERS

(a) Convert €250 to pounds sterling.

(a)

(b) Convert €150 to Norwegian krone.

(b)

(c) Convert €75 to US dollars.

(c)

(d) Convert €25 to Japanese yen.

(d)

(e) Convert €350 to pounds sterling.

(e)

(f) Convert 25,000 yen to euro.

(f)

(g) Convert 2,000 US dollars to euro.

(g)

(h) Convert 4,000 Norwegian krone to euro.

(h)

(i) Convert 8,000 yen to euro.

(i)

(j) Convert 6,000 pounds sterling to euro.

(j)

8 In each space below, write the most appropriate word or term from the following list:

CHOICE   INDUSTRIAL PRODUCE   IMPORT   TRADES   CURRENCY   RAW MATERIALS
(One of the words/terms above does not complete any of the sentences below.)

Paper, oil and wood are examples of .... that we import. Our

major exports are .... from factories. Exporting earns us the

foreign .... that we need to pay for imports. Ireland .... with

over a hundred countries. Foreign trade gives Irish people a greater .... in

what we buy.

9 Draft the balance of trade and the balance of payments from the
following information. Say whether there is a surplus or deficit.

Visible Exports, €10 billion
Invisible Exports, €24 billion
Visible Imports, €14 billion
Invisible Imports, €9 billion

Try a test on this topic

Balance of Trade and Balance of Payments				
	Visible Trade		**€ billion**	**€ billion**
	Exports			
	Less Imports			
Balance of Trade				
Invisible Trade				
	Exports			
	Less Imports			
Invisible Balance				
Balance of Payments				

10 Draft the balance of trade and the balance of payments from the following information. Say if
there is a surplus or deficit.

Visible Exports, €12 billion
Invisible Exports, €27 billion
Visible Imports, €15 billion
Invisible Imports, €11 billion

Balance of Trade and Balance of Payments				
			€ billion	**€ billion**

Chapter 13

Forms of *business*

1 Find the following words hidden in this grid:

Public ✓

Private

Sole

Franchise

Co-operative

Limited

Liable

Control

Profit

Owner

```
F  R  A  N  C  H  I  S  E  P  O  C  E
M  I  P  T  E  T  A  E  O  R  T  V  R
I  V  F  R  A  N  P  U  B  L  I  C  A
T  A  O  C  O  N  T  R  I  T  E  O  T
A  T  E  D  P  F  R  M  A  F  P  F  I
F  E  L  S  R  A  I  R  C  R  R  R  V
R  U  B  A  S  T  E  T  I  A  E  A  E
A  B  A  C  E  P  R  V  E  N  V  N  R
N  N  I  D  O  L  A  R  W  C  A  C  O
C  E  L  O  R  T  N  O  C  H  T  H  I
H  R  C  L  E  R  A  P  R  I  H  I  S
```

2 State **four** examples of state-owned businesses.

(i) ....

(ii) ....

(iii) ....

(iv) ....

3 Explain **two** reasons why state-owned businesses exist in Ireland.

(i)

....

....

....

(ii)

....

....

....

4 Complete the following report using the most appropriate word from the following list:

> SOLE   SHAREHOLDERS   DIRECTORS   OBJECTIVE   PROFIT
> STATE   DIVIDEND   SMALL   AGM   FRANCHISE   LIABILITY
> *(One of the words above does not complete any of the sentences below.)*

The main .... of most businesses is to make a .... Some

firms are owned by a ....trader. These have unlimited .... and are

usually............................businesses. Bigger companies have many............................... . They

meet once a year at the............................ to elect a board of .... If the business

is making a profit they are given a .... Very big firms, like the ESB, are owned by

the ....

5 What do the following letters stand for? *(Write **each** answer in full in the space provided.)*

VAT	
AGM	
LTD	
TTA	

6 Explain the term **Private Sector**:

....

....

....

7 Tick (✓) to show whether each of the following is in the public or private sector:

	PUBLIC	PRIVATE
ESB		
Dunnes Stores Ltd		
Bord Gáis		
McDonald's		
Bishopstown Credit Union		

8 Column 1 is a list of words and phrases. Column 2 is a list of descriptions which can be matched to these words and phrases. *(One description cannot be matched.)*

Column 1	Column 2
Words and phrases	**Descriptions**

1. Sole trader
2. Shareholders
3. Co-operative
4. Limited liability
5. Dividend
6. Objectives
7. AGM
8. Profit
9. Public sector
10. Capital

A. The credit union
B. The amount of profit given to shareholders
C. A meeting held once a year
D. Businesses in the private sector aim to make this
E. State-owned companies
F. One-person business
G. Aims or plans
H. The money invested in a business by the owners
I. They own part of a company
J. The managing director in a company
K. The shareholders can only lose the amount invested

Match the two lists by placing the letter of the most appropriate description under the relevant number below:

1.	2.	3.	4.	5.	6.	7.	8.	9.	10.

9 Tick (✓) whether each of the following is true or false:

	TRUE	FALSE
McDonald's is an example of a private limited company.		
The owners of a McDonald's restaurant have limited liability.		
The local credit union is a private limited company.		
A co-op is owned by its members.		
The members in a credit union do not have limited liability.		

10 Complete this table below using the words in the list:

Limited

Sole

Public

Credit

....	TRADER
....	UNION
....	LIABILITY
....	SECTOR

11 Complete this table to show the differences between the forms of business:

	Sole Trader	Private Limited Company	Co-operative	State Company
Size	SMALL			
Examples				ESB, RTÉ
Liability		LIMITED		
Finance	SAVINGS AND LOANS			
Control			MANAGEMENT COMMITTEE	
Ownership		2–50 SHAREHOLDERS		
Risk			SHARED	
Profits	OWNER GETS ALL THE PROFIT			

Chapter 14
Private limited *company*

1 Name two documents sent into the Companies Registration Office when forming a company.

(i) ....

(ii) ....

2 Explain the following terms:

(i) Certificate of Incorporation

....

....

(ii) Limited Liability

....

....

....

3 Tick (✓) the correct box in each case below.

	TRUE	FALSE
The Memorandum of Association shows the internal rules of the company.		
The Articles of Association shows the number of shares each shareholder has bought.		
Assets are always equal to liabilities.		
The Issued Share Capital is the maximum amount of shares that can be issued.		
A Certificate of Incorporation is issued by the Revenue Commissioners.		

On 1 June last year, John Regan of 22 Moy Road, Ballina, Co. Mayo and Nuala Murray of 31 Straide Road, Castlebar, Co. Mayo formed a private limited company called Castina Ltd.

The objective of the company is to create websites for customers.

The authorised share capital of the company is 100,000 ordinary shares of €1 each. John purchased 20,000 shares and Nuala purchased 10,000.

Complete the memorandum of association for the company below:

Memorandum of Association

COMPANY DETAILS

The name of the company is: ....

The objects for which the company is established are: ....

....

The liability of the members is limited.

The authorised share capital of the company is € .... divided

into .... shares @ €1 each.

We, the several persons whose names, addresses and descriptions are subscribed wish to be formed into a company in pursuance of the Memorandum of Association and we agree to take the number of shares in the capital of the company set opposite our names.

Name, address of each subscriber	Number of shares taken by each subscriber
....	....
....	....
....	....

Date

On 1 May last year Nora Martin, 5 Marino Close, Bray, Co. Wicklow and Joseph O'Connor, 14 Strand Road, Bray, Co. Wicklow formed a private limited company called Educu Books Ltd. They prepared a Memorandum of Association and sent it with all the necessary documents to the Registrar of Companies.

The objectives of the company are to publish and sell educational books. The authorised share capital of Educu Books Ltd is 100,000 €1 ordinary shares.

On 12 May Nora Martin and Joseph O'Connor purchased 25,000 €1 ordinary shares each. The money received from the issue of the shares was lodged to the company bank account.

(i) Complete the memorandum of association for the company below:

Memorandum of Association

COMPANY DETAILS

The name of the company is: ....

The objects for which the company is established are: ....

....

The liability of the members is limited.

The authorised share capital of the company is € .... divided

into .... shares @ €1 each.

We, the several persons whose names, addresses and descriptions are subscribed wish to be formed into a company in pursuance of the Memorandum of Association and we agree to take the number of shares in the capital of the company set opposite our names.

Name, address of each subscriber	Number of shares taken by each subscriber
....	....
....	....
....	....

Date

On 1 May last year Maria Burke of 4 Bridge Street, Athlone, Co. Westmeath and Mike Mitchell of 10 Shannon View, Athlone, Co. Westmeath formed a private limited company called At Your Service Ltd. They prepared a Memorandum of Association and sent it and all the other necessary documents to the Registrar of Companies. A Certificate of Incorporation was then issued.

The objective of the company is to provide computer and secretarial services.
The authorised share capital of At Your Service Ltd is 80,000 €1 ordinary shares.

On 10 May Maria Burke purchased 20,000 shares and Mike Mitchell purchased 15,000 shares. The money received from the issue of these shares was lodged to the company bank account.

(a) Complete the memorandum of association for the company below:

Memorandum of Association

COMPANY DETAILS

The name of the company is: ....

The objects for which the company is established are: ....

....

The liability of the members is limited.

The authorised share capital of the company is € .... divided

into .... shares @ €1 each.

We, the several persons whose names, addresses and descriptions are subscribed wish to be formed into a company in pursuance of the Memorandum of Association and we agree to take the number of shares in the capital of the company set opposite our names.

Name, address of each subscriber	Number of shares taken by each subscriber
....	....
....	....
....	....

Date

(b) Explain **two** advantages of forming a private limited company.

(i)

....

....

(ii)

....

....

(c) Name **two** other documents which should be sent to the Registrar of Companies when forming a private limited company.

(i)

....

(ii)

....

(d) Record the issue of shares in At Your Service Ltd in the accounts below:

Dr			Bank Account				Cr
Date	Details	F	Total	Date	Details	F	Total
			€				€
			Ordinary Share Capital Account				
			€				€

(e) Prepare the opening balance sheet of At Your Service Ltd below:

	Balance Sheet as at 10 May			
	Current Assets			
	Financed by			

7 What do the following letters stand for? *(Write **each** answer in full in the space provided.)*

AGM	
Dr	
Cr	

8 Column 1 is a list of words and phrases. Column 2 is a list of descriptions which can be matched to these words and phrases. *(One description cannot be matched.)*

Column 1
Words and phrases

1. Authorised share capital
2. Issued share capital
3. Certificate of incorporation
4. Memorandum of association
5. Articles of association
6. AGM
7. Assets
8. Liabilities
9. Balance sheet
10. Debit

Column 2
Descriptions

A. This gives a company limited liability
B. This shows the company's name, address and objectives
C. A meeting held once a year
D. The actual amount of shares sold
E. This shows the assets and liabilities of the business
F. Money owed by the business
G. The left-hand side of a ledger account
H. The maximum amount of capital a company may issue
I. The resources of a company
J. The people who own the company
K. This shows the election procedure and voting rights

Match the two lists by placing the letter of the most appropriate description under the relevant number below:

1.	2.	3.	4.	5.	6.	7.	8.	9.	10.

Try a test on this topic

1 Outline two reasons why a company would prepare a business plan:

(i)

....

....

(ii)

....

....

2 Complete the following cash flow forecast.

	A	B	C	D	E	F
		Jan	**Feb**	**Mar**	**Apr**	**TOTAL**
1						
2	**RECEIPTS**					
3	Sales	25,000	25,000	25,000	25,000	
4	Loan				10,000	
5	**A> TOTAL RECEIPTS**					
6						
7	**PAYMENTS**					
8	Cash purchases	9,000	9,000	9,000	9,000	
9	Wages	12,000	12,000	12,000	12,000	
10	Rent	2,000	2,000	2,000	2,000	
11	Light and heat		1,000		900	
12	Motor vehicles			14,000		
13	**B> TOTAL PAYMENTS**					
14	**C> Net Cash (A-B)**					
15	**D> Opening balance**	2,000				
16	**E> Closing balance (C+D)**					

3 Complete the following cash flow forecast.

	A	B	C	D	E	F
1		**May**	**June**	**July**	**August**	**TOTAL**
2	**RECEIPTS**					
3	Sales	30,000	30,000	30,000	30,000	
4	Loan			15,000		
5	**A> TOTAL RECEIPTS**					
6	**PAYMENTS**					
7	Cash purchases	10,000	10,000	10,000	10,000	
8	Wages	15,000	25,000	15,000	15,000	
9	Rent	3,000	3,000	4,000	4,000	
10	**B> TOTAL PAYMENTS**					
11	C> Net Cash (A-B)					
12	D> Opening balance	1,000				
13	E> Closing balance (C+D)					

4 A group of students email a local businesswoman and ask for advice on running their minicompany. Complete the email they get back using words from the list.

> PAYMENTS   STARVED   PROFIT   FUNDS   PRODUCTION   FLOW   RECEIPTS
> *(One of the words above does not complete any of the sentences below.)*

From: sheila@sodco.ie
To: kmsj@gmail.com
Subject: Advice on running your minicompany

Greetings Kevin, Mary, Sarah and Jack,

It sounds like you have a good idea for your business. However, you must be careful not to run out of money. A company which runs short of money is said to be cash _____ . A cash _____ is a plan of company receipts and payments and is worth preparing as it will help you control the money. Wages and other expenses should be listed as _____ in the financial plan of your company. Sales are shown as _____ of the business. Loans are a major source of _____ for most businesses but you may not be able to get any. Finally, remember there is a big difference between _____ and cash.

Best of luck with your minicompany!

Sheila O'Dwyer

5 Lauren (four shares), Keith (three shares) and Mike (three shares) start a school minicompany cleaning cars. Here is their cash flow forecast for the first four weeks.

	A	B	C	D	E	F
1		Week 1	Week 2	Week 3	Week 4	TOTAL
2	**RECEIPTS**					
3	Sales	50	50	50	50	200
4	**A> TOTAL RECEIPTS**	50	50	50	50	200
5						
6	**PAYMENTS**					
7	Sponges	5				5
8	Buckets	15				15
9	Hire of pressure washer	30	30	30	30	120
10	Car wax	10				10
11	Car wash concentrate	5				5
12	**B> TOTAL PAYMENTS**	65	30	30	30	155
13	C> Net Cash (A-B)	(15)	20	20	20	45
14	D> Opening balance	20	5	25	45	20
15	E> Closing balance (C+D)	5	25	45	65	65

(a) What are the total sales for the company? ....

(b) What are the total expenses for the company? ....

(c) Why are the expenses so high in week one? ....

(d) If the €20 opening balance came from the sale of shares, how much is one share? ....

(e) What is their profit at the end of the four weeks? ....

(f) If the profit is to be divided among the shareholders, how much will each get?

Lauren .... Keith .... Mike ....

(g) Which expressions in the cash flow mean the following? ....

   (i)   Income. ....

   (ii) Expenditure. ....

   (iii) Income minus expenditure. ....

   (iv) Cash at the start of the month. ....

   (v)   Cash at the end of the month. ....

Tom and Mary are going to start an electrical shop. Prepare a cash flow forecast for the first four months of the year given the following information:

- Opening cash in hand is €1,000.

Planned income:
- Sales of electrical goods are expected to be €3,000 per month.
- Receipts from repairs are expected to be €500 each month.

Planned expenditure:
- Repayments on van loan will cost €250 per month.
- Shop insurance premium amounts to €150 per year payable in January.
- Electrical bills are expected to be €200 in February and €300 in April.
- Rent will cost €300 per month.
- The telephone bill is expected to be €130 in February and €140 in April.
- Wages are expected to be €2,000 per month.

	A	B	C	D	E	F
		Jan	**Feb**	**Mar**	**Apr**	**TOTAL**
1		Jan	Feb	Mar	Apr	TOTAL
2	**RECEIPTS**					
3	Sales					
4	Repairs					
5	**A> TOTAL RECEIPTS**					
6	**PAYMENTS**					
7	Repayment of loan					
8	Shop insurance					
9	Electricity bills					
10	Rent					
11	Telephone bills					
12	Wages					
13	**B> TOTAL PAYMENTS**					
14	C> Net Cash (A-B)					
15	D> Opening balance					
16	E> Closing balance (C+D)					

Patrick is a lobster exporter. He has advance orders (sales) from European customers for the next four months as follows: May €2,000, June €3,400, July €5,700, August €7,200. He estimates that his expenses over the next few months will be as follows:

- Wages are expected to be €1,500 each month.
- Rent will be €250 per month.
- Electricity bills are expected to be €140 in June and €110 in August.
- The telephone bill is expected to be €150 in June and €170 in August.
- Factory insurance premium is estimated at €240 per year, payable monthly.
- He has opening cash in hand of €750.

(a) Make out a cash flow forecast for this business for May, June, July and August.

	A	B	C	D	E	F
		May	June	July	August	TOTAL
1						
2	**RECEIPTS**					
3	Sales					
4						
5	**A> TOTAL RECEIPTS**					
6	**PAYMENTS**					
7	Wages					
8	Rent					
9	Electricity bills					
10	Telephone bills					
11	Factory insurance					
12	**B> TOTAL PAYMENTS**					
13	C> Net Cash (A-B)					
14	D> Opening balance					
15	E> Closing balance (C+D)					

(b) In which months is there a cash shortage?

(c) Suggest how he might improve his cash flow.

Mary Burke and John Smyth decided to set up a sandwich making and delivery business. The name of their company is SAMBOS Ltd, located at 25 Low Street, Kells, Co. Meath. They have an account in the Bank of Ireland, Kells.

Mary Burke is managing director and John Smyth is the production manager.

Their market research has provided the following information:
- there are 2,000 potential customers;
- there are four businesses in the area supplying sandwiches but none of them offers a delivery service;
- they estimate that they can sell 500 sandwiches per day at €2.65 each.

They estimate their costs as follows: equipment €5,500; delivery van €12,000; lease of premises €14,000; working capital €7,500.

They have savings of €5,500 to invest in the business and can obtain a grant of €10,000 if they produce a business plan. They seek your help in preparing this plan.

(a) Calculate the amount of money they would need to borrow to set up this business.

ANSWER	WORKINGS

(b) Outline **three** suitable methods of advertising and promoting their sandwiches.

(i)

(ii)

(iii)

(c) Complete the business plan on the opposite page using today's date.

Business Plan

COMPANY DETAILS

Name of company ....

Address of company ....

Directors **(i)** .... **(ii)** ....

Marketing Director ....

Production Manager ....

Company Bank ....

PRODUCT/SERVICE

Description ....

MARKET RESEARCH

Size of market ....

Competitors ....

Price per unit **€** ....

SALES PROMOTION

Three suitable methods **(i)** ....

(ii) ....

(iii) ....

FINANCE

Total required **€** ....

Amount available **€** ....

Loan required **€** ....

SIGNED **(i)** .... **(ii)** ....

DATE ....

9. Complete the cash flow forecast below for MHC Ltd. The following additional information should be taken into account:
- Monthly cash sales are expected to increase by 25% beginning in July.
- MHC Ltd expects to receive a loan of €120,000 in May.
- Purchases are expected to remain the same every month.
- Light and heat is expected to decrease by 25% in the months of May and July.
- Wages are expected to remain the same, except in May, where an additional bonus of €12,000 will be paid.
- New motor vehicles will be purchased in May for €125,000.
- Shareholders will be paid a dividend of €14,000 in July.
- Rent is expected to remain the same every month.

Try a test on this topic

	A	B	C	D	E	F	G	H
1		Feb	Mar	Apr	May	June	July	TOTAL
2	RECEIPTS							
3	Sales	80,000	80,000					
4	Loan							
5	A> TOTAL RECEIPTS	80,000	80,000					
6								
7	PAYMENTS							
8	Cash purchases	30,000	30,000					
9	Light and heat		12,000					
10	Wages	25,000	25,000					
11	Motor vehicles							
12	Dividend							
13	Rent	2,000	2,000					
14	B> TOTAL PAYMENTS	57,000	69,000					
15	C> Net Cash (A-B)	23,000	11,000					
16	D> Opening balance	1,000	24,000	35,000				
17	E> Closing balance (C+D)	24,000	35,000					

1 Complete the word grid with the types of finance described below.

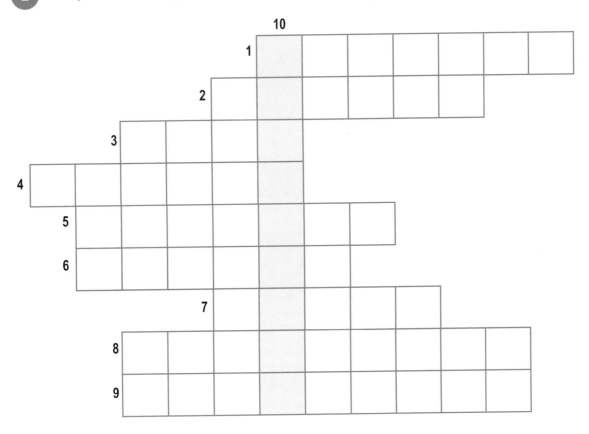

1. This is the money put into the firm by the owners.
2. A successful company will use its capital to make this.
3. _____ purchase is a popular way for a business to acquire vehicles.
4. _____ expenses are not a good source of funds.
5. This is like renting.
6. These are available from Enterprise Ireland or the County Enterprise Boards.
7. These can be long, medium or short.
8. This is a short-term loan given to people with current accounts.
9. Sale and _____ is a good way to get a cash injection into a business.
10. These are your suppliers.

2 Complete the gaps in the table below.

	draft
Sale and	....
....	expenses
Hire	....
....	funds
Long	....
....	profit

3 Use words from the table above to complete this fax.

FAX

To: Robert Moore
From: Carol Synott
RE: Sources of finance

We nearly have all the finance ready. The .... loan will

finance the purchase of the premises and we can use our .... to

pay for the equipment.

Instead of renting I'm going to buy the vans using ....

Today I arranged an .... at the bank to pay for any sudden

expenses we might have during the year.

If the business does well then we can use the .... to pay for

the building of the extension you were talking about.

We could consider sale and .... to give us a cash injection.

4 Calculate which is cheaper for a €6,000 loan.
(a) A term loan if the repayments are €30 per month per €1,000 borrowed over three years.
(b) A hire purchase arrangement for two years if the repayments are €280 per month.

ANSWER	WORKINGS

5 Slaney Ltd gets a €12,000 loan from Bank of Ireland. Record the receipt of the loan to Slaney Ltd in the accounts below:

Dr			Bank Account				Cr
Date	Details	F	Total	Date	Details	F	Total
			€				€
Bank of Ireland Loan Account							
			€				€

6 Match the business needs below with an appropriate loan.

Business Needs	Loan
1. A €250,000 extension to a factory	A. Overdraft
2. Three new delivery vans	B. Creditors
3. Extra stocks of toys for the Christmas market	C. Long-term loan
4. Paying staff wages this week	D. Hire purchase

1.	2.	3.	4.

7 Tick (✓) the appropriate box to indicate whether each of the sources of finance listed below is short-term, medium-term or long-term.

Sources of finance	Short-term	Medium-term	Long-term
Mortgage loan			
Bank overdraft			
Hire purchase loan			

Harry's Electrical Shop got the following details about a €22,000 delivery van.

Term loan from Quick Finance Ltd: €35 per month per €1,000 borrowed for three years.

Leasing: €180 per week.

Try a test on this topic

8 What is the total cost of the term loan?

ANSWER	WORKINGS

9 How much would it cost to lease the van for three years?

ANSWER	WORKINGS

10 Which type of term loan would Harry's need? ....

11 If they decide to get the term loan on 27 November, how would this be recorded in their ledger accounts?

Dr			Bank Account				Cr
Date	Details	F	Total	Date	Details	F	Total
			€				€
			Ulster Bank Loan Account				
			€				€

Chapter 17
Commercial banks

1 Match the bank services below with an appropriate explanation. *(One explanation cannot be matched.)*

Bank Service	Explanation
1. Overdraft	A. Where you save money
2. Deposit account	B. A handy way to pay your car loan
3. Paypath	C. Given to customers with current accounts
4. Standing order	D. A handy way to pay electricity bills
	E. A convenient way to pay wages

1.	2.	3.	4.

2 In each space below, write the most appropriate word from the following list:

REPAID   ORDER   MEMORANDUM   DIRECT   GIRO   NIGHT   DEPOSIT   LOAN   TERM
(One of the words above does not complete any of the sentences below.)

(i) A bank .... is used to transfer money directly from one bank account to another.

(ii) A standing .... is used to pay bills that are the same each month.

(iii) A loan will usually be given to a customer who has .... previous loans.

(iv) Money saved in a .... account earns interest.

(v) Banks provide long-, medium- and short- .... loans to the right customers.

(vi) When a company is opening a current account, the .... of association must be shown to the bank.

(vii) Customers making lodgments outside normal banking hours can arrange to use the .... safe.

(viii) A .... debit is used where the amount of the bill varies each month.

Boyne Ltd is a sportswear manufacturer operating from the Valley Industrial Estate, Drogheda, Co. Louth. The company directors are Ger Byrne and Janice Moore. It owns premises worth €700,000 and has machinery and delivery vans valued at €180,000. The weekly income for the company is €40,000 and the directors feel this can be increased if the company could get a ten-year loan to build an extension to the factory costing €200,000 and purchase new machinery costing €80,000. The company has reserves of €50,000 and is eligible for a €40,000 grant.

3 How much of a loan does Boyne Ltd above require?

ANSWER	WORKINGS

4 Boyne Ltd applied for a ten-year loan from Ulster Bank. Complete the loan application form below using today's date.

Ulster Bank
LOAN APPLICATION FORM

COMPANY DETAILS

Company name	
Address	
Names of directors	
Nature of business	
Annual income	

LOAN REQUIRED

Amount	
Purpose	
How long do you want the loan for?	
What security is available?	

SIGNATURES	DATE

5 Record the receipt of the loan to Boyne Ltd in the accounts below:

Dr			Bank Account				Cr
Date	Details	F	Total	Date	Details	F	Total
			€				€
		Ulster Bank Loan Account					
			€				€

6 Jim Daly, 13 Island View, Clifden, has a current account, no. 16547653, in Bank of Ireland, Westport branch. On 11 March he lodged to his account a cheque for €700 and €800 in notes. Complete the lodgment form.

LODGMENT RECORD	**Lodgment** Please specify account: Current ☐ Savings ☐ Other ☐		
Name(s)	Name(s)		Notes
	Address		Coin
€	Date 20		Total Cash
	Paid in by		Cheques
Please specify account Current ☐ Savings ☐ Other ☐	Cashier's Stamp and Initials	Customer's Account Number	Total

7 List **three** items a business must provide to the bank when opening a current account.

(i) ....

(ii) ....

(iii) ....

8 Explain the term **Paypath**:

....

....

....

Donna Summers, 26 Seapoint, Cobh, has a current account, no. 14256106, in AIB, Cork branch. She received a four-year loan of €20,000 from her bank to buy a delivery van. Terms of the loan agreement were:
- capital repayments of €5,000 each year
- interest 12% APR.

eTest.ie
Try a test on this topic

9 Calculate the total interest payable over the four years.

ANSWER	WORKINGS

10 On 10 June she lodged to her account a cheque for €700 and €800 in notes. Complete the lodgment form.

LODGMENT RECORD

Name(s)

€

Please specify account
Current ☐   Savings ☐
Other ☐

Lodgment
Please specify account: Current ☐   Savings ☐   Other ☐

Name(s)

Address

Date   20

Paid in by

Cashier's Stamp
and Initials

Customer's Account Number

Notes
Coin
Total Cash
Cheques
Total

11 On 23 June she withdrew €250 from her account. Complete the withdrawal form.

Withdrawal   Branch Number   Account Number

Current Deposit Cashsave

Brand/Initials

Branch
Received the sum of

Signed
Address
Narrative

€

For joint Savings Accounts
I certify that all parties in the
account are alive on this date

Date
Signed

Chapter 18

Business *insurance*

1 For each of the businesses listed below, identify one possible risk from the list on the right, as in the example.

BUSINESS	RISKS
1. Supermarket	A. Petrol going on fire
2. Chocolate manufacturer	B. Freezer breaking down
3. Meat exporter	C. Bricks falling on passers-by
4. Garage	D. Trawler sunk by submarine
5. Builder	E. Armed raid
6. Bank	F. Damage to car
7. Farmer	G. Sweets making a consumer ill
8. Car hire company	H. Shop window broken by vandals
9. Ice cream company	I. Foreign customer not paying up
10. Fisherman	J. Sheep killed by dogs

2 Answer true or false to the statements below. You may need to revise Chapter 9 first.
(Tick (✓) the most appropriate box.)

	TRUE	FALSE
You must tell the truth when you apply for insurance.		
Any risk can be insured.		
You always get the full amount you claim.		
If your €5,000 car is stolen you can claim €6,000.		
You cannot insure your local bank against robbery.		
Car insurance is compulsory.		
You can insure your factory with two different companies.		
If you are underinsured you may not get the full amount you claim.		

NPD Electric Ltd, 34 Live Wire Drive, Galway manufactures and distributes electrical appliances for the home. It sells its products in Ireland.
NPD Electric Ltd wishes to review its insurance policies and requires advice on its insurance requirements. It supplies the following information.

Its assets include: Premises; Equipment; Motor Vehicles; Stock of electrical appliances. It has 80 employees.
NPD Electric Ltd lodges its cash twice weekly in a bank ten kilometres away.

3 Name **two** types of insurance that NPD Electric Ltd is required to have by law.

(i)
....

(ii)
....

4 Name **four other** relevant types of insurance you would advise it to have and the reasons for having these.

(i)
....

Reason:
....

(ii)
....

Reason:
....

(iii)
....

Reason:
....

(iv)
....

Reason:
....

5 Why is it important for NPD Electric Ltd to have adequate insurance?

....

....

....

6 Assume you are Martina Toban, Insurance Consultant, 10 Castle View, Roscommon.
Complete the following report, on today's date, for the directors of NPD Electric Ltd, setting out the following:
  (i)   two types of insurance that NPD Electric Ltd is required to have by law
  (ii) four other relevant types of insurance you would advise it to have and the reasons for having these
  (iii) the importance of having adequate insurance for NPD Electric Ltd.

BUSINESS REPORT

10 Castle View
Roscommon

To:
_____

_____

_____

Date: _____

Here is my report on the insurance requirements for NPD Electric Ltd. Here are the main findings:

Compulsory insurance:
_____

_____

Other insurance:
_____

_____

_____

_____

Adequate insurance:
_____

_____

_____

Please contact me to discuss any aspect of this report.

Signed: _____

Title: _____

Haircare Ltd wants to insure the following: buildings €200,000; machinery €80,000; two vans at €14,000 each; stock €60,000; office cash €2,500.

They got the following quotation from PremiumCover Ltd: insurance for buildings and machinery €4 per €1,000 insured; vehicle insurance €900 per van; stock insurance €9 per €1,000 insured; cash insurance €10 per €500 insured. As new clients they are entitled to a 20% discount off the total premium.

Haircare Ltd agreed to take out this insurance on everything at replacement cost (as stated above) except for the buildings, which they insured for €150,000.

7 Calculate the total amount of the premium paid by Haircare Ltd.

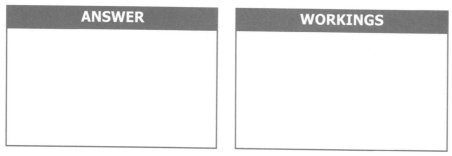

ANSWER	WORKINGS

8 In the event of damage to the buildings of €80,000, how much compensation would Haircare Ltd receive?

ANSWER	WORKINGS

eTest.ie
Try a test on this topic

9 Show how to record the payment of the total premium in the ledger on 2 November.

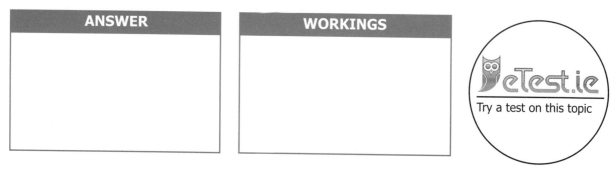

Dr			Bank Account					Cr
Date	Details	F	Total	Date	Details		F	Total
			€					€
			Insurance Account					
			€					€

1 Distinguish between internal and external communication.

Internal communication

....

....

External communication

....

....

....

2 List **four** factors which determine the choice of a form of communication:

(i)

....

(ii)

....

(iii)

....

(iv)

....

3 Find a word in the list to complete each word or phrase in the table:

Business

Post

Phone

Publicity

E

....	Post
Mobile	....
....	mail
Free	....
....	reply service

Midlands Book Supplies Ltd, 63 Shannon Drive, Athlone distributes books and magazines throughout Ireland.
The company wishes to review its methods of communication and requires advice on its requirements. It supplies the following information.

Midlands Book Supplies Ltd has a fleet of 20 vans which deliver throughout Ireland.
It has a head office in Athlone with thirty staff. The company imports magazines and books from around the world.

4 Name **two** types of written communication that Midlands Book Supplies Ltd could use.

(i)
....

(ii)
....

5 Name **three** services operated by An Post that would improve communications between the company and its customers.

(i)
....

Reason:
....

(ii)
....

Reason:
....

(iii)
....

Reason:
....

6 Name **three** services operated by the telecommunications companies that would improve the communications between the company and its customers.

(i)
....

Reason:
....

(ii)
....

Reason:
....

(iii)
....

Reason:
....

7 Assume you are Jenny Nolan, Communications Consultant, 26 Harbour View, Sligo.
Using your notes from the previous page, complete the following report, on today's date, for
the directors of Midlands Book Supplies Ltd, setting out the following:

(i) **two** types of written communication that Midlands Book Supplies Ltd should use

(ii) **three** services operated by An Post that would improve communications between the
company and its customers

(iii) **three** services operated by the telecommunications companies that would improve the
communications between the company and its customers.

BUSINESS REPORT

26 Harbour View
Sligo

To: _____   Date: _____

_____

_____

Here is my report on the communications requirements for Midlands Book Supplies Ltd.
Here are the main findings:

Written communications: _____

_____

_____

An Post: _____

_____

_____

_____

Telecommunications Services: _____

_____

_____

Please contact me to discuss any aspect of this report.

Signed: _____

Title: _____

8 Draw a bar chart to show the following rates of inflation in a country:

Year:	2006	2007	2008	2009	2010
Rate:	2%	5%	9%	3%	6%

9 Draw a line graph to show the following purchases for a company:

Year:	2006	2007	2008	2009	2010
Purchases:	7,000	3,000	5,000	6,000	2,000

10 Draw a pie chart to show the following sales for a company:

	Sales
Ulster	2,000
Munster	6,000
Leinster	12,000
Connacht	4,000

eTest.ie
Try a test on this topic

1 Circle the primary producers from the producers listed below, as in the example.

Clothing firms   Fish farming

(Farmers)   Insurance firms

Doctors   Banking

Forestry firms   Mining firms

Furniture firms   New technology firms

2 Fill in the two blank spaces in the following chain of distribution.

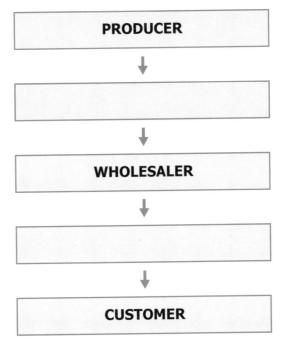

```
┌─────────────────────────────┐
│          PRODUCER           │
└─────────────────────────────┘
               ↓
┌─────────────────────────────┐
│                             │
└─────────────────────────────┘
               ↓
┌─────────────────────────────┐
│         WHOLESALER          │
└─────────────────────────────┘
               ↓
┌─────────────────────────────┐
│                             │
└─────────────────────────────┘
               ↓
┌─────────────────────────────┐
│          CUSTOMER           │
└─────────────────────────────┘
```

3 Distinguish between independent retailers and department stores.

Independent retailers

....

....

Department stores

....

4 Find a word in the list to complete each phrase in the table:

Store

Independent

Vending

Order

Cash

....	retailer
Mail	....
....	and carry
Voluntary	....
....	machine

5 List **four** functions of a retailer:

(i)

....

(ii)

....

(iii)

....

(iv)

....

6 In each space below, write the most appropriate word from the following list:

WHOLESALER MANUFACTURER CONSUMER VOLUNTARY SHOPKEEPERS BULK DELIVER
(One of the words above does not complete any of the sentences below.)

(i) Spar is an example of a .... store.

(ii) Wholesalers buy in .... from manufacturers.

(iii) Wholesalers supply the .... with market information.

(iv) Traditional wholesalers .... the goods to the retailer.

(v) The .... is the middleman between the manufacturer and retailers.

(vi) Cash-and-carry wholesalers require .... to collect their own goods.

7 Tick (✓) whether each of the following is true or false:

	TRUE	FALSE
All products must be sold to a wholesaler before going to the retailer.		
Wholesalers buy in bulk and sell in smaller amounts to shops.		
All wholesalers will deliver goods to the shops.		
An ordinary consumer can buy goods from a wholesaler.		
Cash-and-carry wholesalers give credit.		
Easons is an example of a wholesaler.		
Centra is an example of a voluntary store.		

8 List **three** services of a wholesaler to the retailer:

(i)
....

(ii)
....

(iii)
....

9 Fill in the two blank spaces in the following chain of distribution.

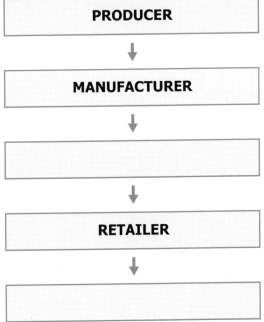

10 Column 1 is a list of words and phrases. Column 2 is a list of descriptions which can be matched to these words and phrases. *(One description cannot be matched.)*

Column 1	Column 2
Words and phrases	**Descriptions**
1. Consumer	A. Sells goods to the shops for resale
2. Wholesaler	B. Many different shops in one building
3. Retailer	C. A store that sells goods through the post only
4. Supermarket	D. Large shop divided into separate units
5. Mail order	E. Buys goods for private use
6. Department store	F. Large self-service shop
7. Shopping centre	G. Sells goods to the public for private use
	H. Makes goods for the public

Match the two lists by placing the letter of the most appropriate description under the relevant number below:

1.	2.	3.	4.	5.	6.	7.

11 Explain the term **Tertiary Producers**:

....

....

....

....

....

Try a test on this topic

Chapter 21
People at work

1 Explain the term **Work**:

....

....

....

2 Distinguish between employment and unemployment.

Employment

....

....

....

Unemployment

....

....

....

3 List **three** causes of unemployment:

(i)
....

(ii)
....

(iii)
....

4 Explain the term **Labour Force**:

....

....

....

5 List **three** responsibilities of employees:

(i)

....

(ii)

....

(iii)

....

6 List **three** rights of employees:

(i)

....

(ii)

....

(iii)

....

7 Match the modern trends below with an appropriate explanation. *(One explanation cannot be matched.)*

Modern Trends	Explanation
1. Term time	A. Employee works from home
2. Job sharing	B. Employee works any forty hours during the week
3. Teleworking	C. Two or more workers share one full-time position
	D. Employee does not work during school breaks

1.	2.	3.

8 Tick (✓) whether each of the following is true or false in relation to the labour force.

The labour force includes:	TRUE	FALSE
Old age pensioners		
University students		
Unemployed people seeking employment		
All unemployed people		

9 In each space below, write the most appropriate word or term from the following list:

> UNEMPLOYED   AGRICULTURE   SERVICE   RESPONSIBILITIES
> SIXTEEN   RIGHTS   SELF-EMPLOYED
> *(One of the words/terms above does not complete any of the sentences below.)*

(i) All workers have certain obligations and ....

(ii) Most people are employed in .... companies and very few work in ....

(iii) You must be .... years of age to work in most firms.

(iv) If you don't work for someone you could start your own business and be ....

(v) If you still have no job you will be ....

10 Fill in the two blank spaces in the following organisation chart.

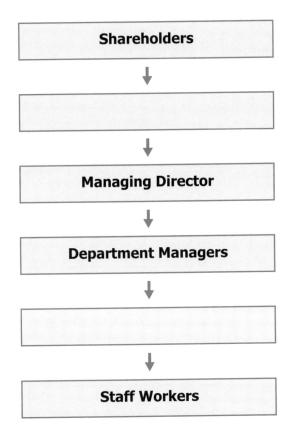

11 Explain the term **Entrepreneur**:

....

....

....

12 List **three** characteristics of self-employment:

(i)
....

(ii)
....

(iii)
....

13 List **three** rewards of self-employment:

(i)
....

(ii)
....

(iii)
....

14 Find a word in the list to complete each phrase in the table:

Managing

Job

Term

Employed

Force

....	Sharing
Self	....
....	Director
Labour	....
....	Time

Open for Business *Workbook*

Chapter 22
Being an *employer*

Activity 22.2 Calculate wages Question 2

In these questions you have to work out the PAYE and PRSI before you find the net pay and complete a payslip.

(a) Shane Dwyer is paid €12 per hour and last week he worked 21 hours. His tax credits are €50 per week. His rate of tax is 25%, PRSI is 5% of gross and his other weekly deduction is health insurance €12.

Wages Slip:				Week:	
PAY	**€**	**DEDUCTIONS**	**€**	**NET PAY**	
Basic		PAYE			
Overtime		PRSI		**€**	
		Other			
GROSS PAY		**TOTAL DEDUCTIONS**			

(b) Janette Kearns is paid €546 for a 39-hour week and €21 per hour for overtime. Last week she worked 47 hours. Her tax credits are €110 per week. Her rate of tax is 25%, PRSI is 5% of gross and her other weekly deduction is pension €25.

Wages Slip:				Week:	
PAY	**€**	**DEDUCTIONS**	**€**	**NET PAY**	
Basic		PAYE			
Overtime		PRSI		**€**	
		Other			
GROSS PAY		**TOTAL DEDUCTIONS**			

(c) Peter Brennan is paid €468 for a basic 39-hour week and €18 per hour overtime. Last week he worked 49 hours. His tax credits are €96 per week. His rate of tax is 25%, PRSI is 5% of gross and his other weekly deduction is union dues €3.

Wages Slip:				Week:	
PAY	**€**	**DEDUCTIONS**	**€**	**NET PAY**	
Basic		PAYE			
Overtime		PRSI		**€**	
		Other			
GROSS PAY		**TOTAL DEDUCTIONS**			

Lenny: basic pay €370; no overtime; PAYE €55; PRSI €28; health insurance €9.27.
Aisling: basic pay €547; overtime €220; PAYE €146; PRSI €38; pension €12.50.
Kevin: basic pay €190; commission €750; PAYE €184; PRSI €63; union dues €14.67.
The employer's rate of PRSI is 10% of gross pay.

(a) Complete the wages and salaries book.

Date	Name	Basic Pay	OT/ Comm	Total Gross Pay	PAYE	PRSI	Other	Total Deductions	Net Pay	Employer's PRSI
Dec 1										
	TOTALS									

(b) Complete the cash analysis chart.

Name	Total	€50	€20	€10	€5	€2	€1	50c	20c	10c	5c	2c	1c
Lenny													
Aisling													
Kevin													
TOTALS													

(c) Show the entries in the bank and wages accounts.

Dr			Bank Account				Cr
Date	Details	F	Total	Date	Details	F	Total
			€				€
			Wages Account				
			€				€

Clodagh: basic pay €460; no overtime; PAYE €66; PRSI €34; health insurance €9.26.
Alex: basic pay €840; overtime €230; PAYE €187; PRSI €46; union dues €4.60.
Brian: basic pay €240; commission €820; PAYE €197; PRSI €58; pension €14.68.
The employer's rate of PRSI is 10% of gross pay.

(a) Complete the wages and salaries book.

Date	Name	Basic Pay	OT/ Comm	Total Gross Pay	PAYE	PRSI	Other	Total Deductions	Net Pay	Employer's PRSI
Dec 1										
	TOTALS									

(b) Complete the cash analysis chart.

Name	Total	€50	€20	€10	€5	€2	€1	50c	20c	10c	5c	2c	1c
Clodagh													
Alex													
Brian													
TOTALS													

(c) Show the entries in the bank and wages accounts.

Dr			Bank Account				Cr
Date	Details	F	Total	Date	Details	F	Total
			€				€
			Wages Account				
			€				€

Pauline Kelly, head mechanic in a local garage, resigned from her job and set up her own business called PK Motors. Pauline has employed Austin Martin as an assistant mechanic.

(a) State **two** rewards for Pauline as the owner of PK Motors.

(i) ....

(ii) ....

State **two** risks for Pauline as the owner of PK Motors.

(i) ....

(ii) ....

State **two** rights Pauline has as an employer.

(i) ....

(ii) ....

State **two** responsibilities Pauline has as an employer.

(i) ....

(ii) ....

Explain the importance to PK Motors of keeping employee records.

....

....

(b) Austin Martin will be paid a gross wage of €3,600 per month by PK Motors. He will pay income tax (PAYE) at the rate of 20% on the first €2,450 of his wage and 42% on the remainder. Austin Martin has a tax credit of €238 per month. The employee PRSI rate is 7.5% and the employer's PRSI rate is 12%. Complete the wages book of PK Motors for this month.

Date	Name	Basic Pay	OT/ Comm	Total Gross Pay	PAYE	PRSI	Other	Total Deductions	Net Pay	Employer's PRSI
1 Dec										

Calculate the total cost of employing Austin Martin for the month.

ANSWER	WORKINGS

eTest.ie
Try a test on this topic

Chapter 23
Industrial *relations*

1 Tick (✓) whether each of the following is true or false:

	TRUE	FALSE
SIPTU is the name of a trade union.		
AIB is the name of a trade union.		
INTO is the name of a trade union.		
All employees are obliged to join a trade union.		
A garda can join a trade union.		
There is no army trade union.		
If you get a job in a factory you can join the ASTI trade union.		
The IBOA is a finance union representing bank officials.		
Actors Equity is an example of a craft union.		
The shop steward tries to solve problems before a dispute arises.		

2 Explain the term **Shop Steward**:

....

....

....

3 List **four** benefits of joining a trade union:

  (i)
....

  (ii)
....

  (iii)
....

  (iv)
....

Paul Farrell is the shop steward at Equipment Engineering Ltd. All the workers in this company are members of the trade union, SIPTU. At a recent meeting, they discussed the National Wage Agreement and decided on the position they should take in future agreements.

4 List **three** duties of a shop steward:

(i)

(ii)

(iii)

5 List **three** problems which a worker might bring to the attention of the union:

(i)

(ii)

(iii)

6 Describe **one** course of industrial action, other than a strike, which a union could follow in pursuit of a claim and in solving the dispute.

7 Explain the term **National Wage Agreement**:

The *shop steward* in Valley Textiles Ltd, a clothing company, has asked her union head office to investigate a dispute. The problem concerns Catherine, who maintains that she was overlooked for *promotion*. Catherine's colleagues agree that she should have got the position. They have started a *work-to-rule,* with a view to an *all-out strike.*

The management are concerned that *production* for the Christmas market will be interfered with and want a speedy end to the dispute. They insist, however, that the person they appointed – Richard – is the best one for the job.

8 Explain the italicised words.

Shop steward

....

....

Promotion

....

....

Work-to-rule

....

....

All-out strike

....

....

Production

....

....

9 What steps have been taken so far to resolve this dispute?

....

....

....

....

10 How would a **conciliator** help in resolving this dispute?

....

....

....

Steve, Peter, Ann, Gina and Mike meet at their past pupils' school reunion.

Peter: So how come you managed to get on TV, Ann?

Ann: Oh, I was elected shop steward for my union and I was asked to go to the annual conference in Donegal. We have 220,000 members so it was a great honour.

Gina: I remember that conference, Ann, I was there covering it for my paper. I never saw you – the hotel was so full of delegates. My union only has 3,900 members and our conference is tiny in comparison with yours.

Peter: How many members does your union have, Mike?

Mike: It's against the law for me to join a union. We have a representative association which looks after our pay and conditions. I think we have about 9,000 members.

Peter: You're in a big trade union, Stephen, aren't you?

Steve: Yes, we have 18,000 members in our association. When I was sick last year they were very helpful with information on sick benefits.

Gina: My union gave me terrific information about maternity leave last year when I was having the baby.

Mike: But what about you, Peter, you're asking all the questions. How many members does your union have?

Peter: Our association has 13,000 members, which is slightly smaller than John's union, which has 17,000.

Ann: Speaking of John, didn't he do a great job organising this? He's working here, you know, he never left the place.

11 Study the conversation and answer these questions.

(i) Why was Ann in Donegal?

....

(ii) How did the union help Steve?

....

(iii) How did the union help Gina?

....

(iv) Why isn't Mike a member of a trade union?

....

(v) What type of trade union is Peter in?

....

12 Complete this table, showing the name of the union each friend is a member of.

	Union
Steve	
Peter	
Ann	
Gina	
Mike	
John	

Try a test on this topic

Chapter 24

Sales and *marketing*

1 Explain the term **Target Market**:

....

....

2 Distinguish between **Field Research** and **Desk Research.**

Field Research

....

....

Desk Research

....

....

3 List **three** advertising media:

(i) ....

(ii) ....

(iii) ....

4 Why is **Branding** so important in marketing?

....

....

5 Fill in the two missing parts of the marketing mix in the spaces provided.

PRODUCT			PLACE

6 Explain the term **PR**:

....

....

Mountview Community School, situated five miles from the nearest town, has six hundred students. The school is considering providing hot meals at lunchtime, at a price of €1.50 per meal. Patricia Dooley, Marketing Consultant, carries out a survey and finds the following information:

Total number of students willing to buy the meals   400

Types of hot food preferred by students:

Burger and chips	250
Chicken curry and rice	120
Lasagne and salad	30

Costs of making the meals are as follows:

Food	€0.90 per meal
Other costs	€0.40 per meal

7 Calculate the percentage of students willing to purchase hot meals, and the percentage requiring each different type of meal.

ANSWER	WORKINGS

8 Calculate the daily profit if 400 meals are sold.

ANSWER	WORKINGS

9 List **three** suitable methods of promoting the hot meals in the school:

(i)

....

(ii)

....

(iii)

....

10 Do you recommend the school goes ahead with providing meals? (Give a reason for your answer.)

Recommendation:

....

Reason:

....

11 Assume you are Patricia Dooley, Marketing Consultant, 54 Island Avenue, Clifden, Co. Mayo. Using your notes from the previous page, complete the following report, on today's date, for the board of management of Mountview Community School, setting out the following:

(i) the percentage of students willing to purchase hot meals, and the percentage requiring the different types of meals

(ii) the daily profit if 400 meals are sold

(iii) three suitable methods of promoting the hot meals in the school

(iv) recommendation, with reason, on whether to proceed or not.

BUSINESS REPORT

54 Island Avenue
Clifden, Co. Mayo

To: _____   Date: _____

_____

_____

Here is my report on the provision of hot meals in Mountview Community School. Here are the main findings:

Percentage Wanting Hot Meals: _____

_____

_____

Daily Profit: _____

_____

_____

Methods of Promotion: _____

_____

_____

Recommendation: _____

_____

_____

Please contact me to discuss any aspect of this report.

Signed: _____

Title: _____

12 In each space below, write the most appropriate word from the following list:

ADVERTISE   MEDIA   SLOGAN   ADVERTISERS   TARGET
ADVERTISING   PERSUASIVE   BRAND   ADVERTISEMENTS   MARKET   SAMPLE
(One of the words above does not complete any of the sentences below.)

(i)   Researchers usually survey a .... of their target market.

(ii)   .... advertising tries to convince consumers they need the product.

(iii)   The main advertising .... are newspapers, TV and radio.

(iv)   People often complain about the content of certain ....

(v)   The .... name identifies the product.

(vi)   A .... is a catchy phrase used in an advertisement.

(vii)   .... should act responsibly when making ads.

(viii)   Some magazines allow you to .... for free.

(ix)   Good .... can be entertaining.

(x)   The .... market for petrol is car drivers.

13 Fill in the two missing parts of the marketing mix in the spaces provided.

	PRICE		PLACE

14 Briefly explain each of the following selling techniques.

Special offers

....

....

Free samples

....

....

Loyalty cards

....

....

Loss leaders

....

....

Sponsorship

....

....

Chapter 25

Delivery *systems*

1 Refer to the distance chart on the right. What is the distance between each of the towns listed below?

Towns	Distance
Sligo to Kilkenny	
Galway to Sligo	
Dublin to Clifden	
Kilkenny to Dublin	
Mullingar to Wexford	

Clifden

300	Dublin								
148	230	Ennis							
79	216	70	Galway						
251	120	150	170	Kilkenny					
410	192	375	340	320	Larne				
222	80	160	143	120	210	Mullingar			
352	163	246	274	100	360	200	Rosslare		
170	217	195	140	240	241	135	327	Sligo	
330	142	227	253	80	346	180	20	307	Wexford

2 Briefly explain each of the following factors to consider when choosing a method of delivery.

Cost

Speed

Distance

Reliability

3 Other than roads, name four methods of delivering goods.

(i)

(ii)

(iii)

(iv)

Study the following information for a round trip from Cavan to Cork.

(i)   The annual motor tax is €480.
(ii)   The annual van insurance is €750.
(iii) The annual maintenance costs are €270.
(iv)   It is 300km from Cavan to Cork.
(v)   The driver is paid €100 per day.
(vi)   The van covers 12km per litre of diesel.
(vii) Diesel costs 96 cent a litre.
(viii) The company is open 250 days a year.

4 Calculate the total fixed costs of the round trip from Cavan to Cork.

Fixed costs	€	WORKINGS
Motor tax		
Insurance		
Maintenance		
Total fixed costs		

5 If the company is open 250 days a year, what is the fixed cost for a day?

Fixed cost for a day	WORKINGS

6 Calculate the total variable costs of the round trip from Cavan to Cork.

Variable costs		WORKINGS
Distance		
Diesel used		
Fuel costs		
Labour costs		
Total variable costs		

7 What is the total cost of the journey?

Fixed cost for a day	
Total variable costs	
Cost of journey	

8 Express the total cost of the return journey as a percentage of the invoice value of the goods, given as €3,080.

ANSWER	WORKINGS

9 Give **one** reason why it is important to know this percentage.

....

....

....

10 List **three** costs associated with owning and running a delivery van:

(i)
....

(ii)
....

(iii)
....

11 List **three** advantages of a company owning its own fleet of delivery vans:

(i)
....

(ii)
....

(iii)
....

Dublin Heuston	0525	0710	0830	1050	1320	1520	1710	1835	1915
Newbridge									1941
Kildare			0900						1950
Portarlington					1402				2005
Portlaoise	0616	0800	0925		1414				2019
Ballybrophy			0941						2035
Templemore			0955		1440				2048
Thurles	0651	0836	1009	1211	1454	1644		1956	2103
Limerick Junction	0713	0858	1031	1233	1516	1706	1849		2125
Charleville	0733		1053	1253	1537			2035	2146
Mallow (arrival)	0748	0931	1108	1309	1552	1738	1921	2050	2202
Mallow (departure)	0750	0933	1121	1311	1554	1739	1923	2100	2203
Cork	0819	1001	1149	1339	1622	1807	1951	2130	2231

12 Study the train timetable above and answer these questions.

	ANSWER
What time does the first train for Cork leave Dublin Heuston station?	
What time does the 8.30 a.m. train from Dublin Heuston arrive in Thurles?	
What time does the 1.20 p.m. (13.20) train from Dublin Heuston arrive in Cork?	
What time is the last train to Cork from Dublin Heuston?	
If you travelled on the 7.50 p.m. (19.50) train from Kildare, how long would it take you to get to Charleville?	

13 Tick (✓) an appropriate method of delivery in each of these situations.

		Road	Rail	Air	Sea	Pipes
1	Newspapers from Dublin to Galway					
2	Tweed suits to a customer in Boston					
3	Chocolate to Britain					
4	Butter for the German market					
5	Fresh lobsters to a Japenese customer					
6	Gas from Kinsale to Wexford					
7	Powdered milk to a famine-stricken region					
8	Whiskey for the Italian market					

1 Activity 26.1 Question 3

Music Wholesalers Ltd, Bridge Street, Galway supplies guitars to music shops around Ireland.
On 5 March Music Wholesalers Ltd send a quotation for the following goods to Billy Stafford,
Purchasing Manager, Alto Ltd, Catherine Street, Limerick.

Malaga Guitars (Model MJ35) €45 each
Orlando Guitars (Model OA67) €90 each

From the above details, complete quotation no. 67.

QUOTATION

Quotation no.: 67

Music Wholesalers Ltd
Bridge Street
Galway

Date: _____

_____

_____

_____

Model No.	Description	Price Each €

Computer Wholesalers Ltd, College Street, Waterford supplies computers to shops around Ireland. On 14 April Computer Wholesalers Ltd send a quotation for the following goods to Jen Conroy, Purchasing Manager, PC Ireland Ltd, Morgan Street, Cork.

Mini Laptops (Model ML64)	€150 each
Desktops (Model DT97)	€340 each
Printers (Model P52)	€45 each

From the above details, complete quotation no. 259.

QUOTATION

Quotation no.: 259

Computer Wholesalers Ltd
College Street
Waterford

Date: _____

_____

_____

_____

Model No.	Description	Price Each €

E & O E

3 What do the following letters stand for? *(Write **each** answer in full in the space provided.)*

FOR	
CWO	
COD	

Billy Stafford is the purchasing manager at Alto Ltd, Catherine Street, Limerick. On 27 April he orders the following goods from Music Wholesalers Ltd, Bridge Street, Galway.

10 Malaga Guitars	Model MJ35 @ €45 each
18 Orlando Guitars	Model OA67 @ €90 each

From the above details, complete order no. 241.

ORDER

Order no.: 241

Alto Ltd
Catherine Street
Limerick

Date: _____

_____

_____

_____

Please supply the following goods:

Quantity	Description	Price Each €

Signed: _____

Title: _____

E & O E

5 Tick (✓) whether each of the following is true or false:

	TRUE	FALSE
The customer sends the letter of enquiry		
The customer sends the quotation		
The customer sends the order		

Jen Conroy is the purchasing manager at PC Ireland Ltd, Morgan Street, Cork. On 16 May she orders the following goods from Computer Wholesalers Ltd, College Street, Waterford.

15 Mini Laptops	Model ML64 @ €150 each
20 Desktops	Model DT97 @ €340 each
18 Printers	Model P52 @ €45 each

From the above details, complete order no. 169.

ORDER

Order no.: 169

PC Ireland Ltd
Morgan Street
Cork

Date: _____

_____

_____

_____

Please supply the following goods:

Quantity	Description	Price Each €

Signed: _____

Title: _____

E & O E

---

7 Fill in the two blank spaces to show the sequence of documents used when purchasing goods.

| **Letter of Enquiry** | → | | → | | → | **Invoice** |

Paul Gearon works as a van driver for Haircare Wholesalers Ltd, Cranmore Industrial Estate, Sligo. On 12 March he loaded 10 flat irons, 15 hair dryers and 25 gift sets into his van and delivered them to Mane Hair Ltd, Main Street, Letterkenny. Draft the delivery docket he brought with him.

DELIVERY DOCKET

No.: 186

Haircare Wholesalers Ltd
Cranmore Industrial Estate
Sligo

Date: _____

_____

_____

_____

Please supply the following goods:

Quantity	Description

Received the above goods in good condition

Signed: _____

E & O E

9 What do the following letters stand for? (*Write **each** answer in full in the space provided.*)

E & O E	
VAT	

On 4 April O'Donoghues Song Supplies, Mitchell Street, Tipperary sent an invoice, no. 251, to Cronin's Music Shop, Bowers Lane, Killarney for the following goods: 20 copies of *Irish Songs (IC4)* at €4 each, 60 copies of *Country Songs (CS62)* at €3 each and 10 copies of *Gaelic Songs (GS148)* at €12 each. Trade discount is 20% and VAT is 10%. Draft the invoice sent on 4 April.

INVOICE
No.: 251

O'Donoghues Song Supplies Ltd
Mitchell Street
Tipperary

Date: _____

_____

Quantity	Description	Code	Price Each	Total €

Total (excluding VAT)	
Trade discount	
Subtotal	
VAT	
Total (including VAT)	

E & O E

---

11 Outline how Cronin's Music Shop should treat invoices received.

....

....

....

....

On 9 April Cronin's Music Shop, Bowers Lane, Killarney returned 3 copies of *Gaelic Songs* (faulty covers) at €12 each to O'Donoghues Song Supplies, Mitchell Street, Tipperary. Trade discount is 20% and VAT is 10%. Draft the credit note sent by O'Donoghues Song Supplies on 10 April.

CREDIT NOTE

No.: 125

O'Donoghues Song Supplies Ltd
Mitchell Street
Tipperary

Date: _____

Your Invoice No.: _____

Quantity	Description	Code	Price Each	Total €
			Total (excluding VAT)	
			Trade discount	
			Subtotal	
			VAT	
			Total (including VAT)	

E & O E

13 When is a credit note issued by a seller?

....

....

....

....

On 26 May Baby Supplies Ltd, Castle Street, Thurles, sent an invoice, no. 364, to Bouncy Ltd, School Street, Wexford for the following goods: 15 travel cots (TC86) at €72 each, 20 car seats (CS72) at €84 each and 4 twin pushchairs (TPC8) at €215 each. Trade discount is 20% and VAT is 10%. Draft the invoice sent on 26 May.

INVOICE

No.: 364

Baby Supplies Ltd
Castle Street
Thurles

Date: _____

_____

_____

_____

Quantity	Description	Code	Price Each	Total €

Total (excluding VAT)	
Trade discount	
Subtotal	
VAT	
Total (including VAT)	

E & O E

15 Fill in the two blank spaces to show the sequence of documents used when purchasing goods.

[   ] → **Quotation** → [   ] → **Invoice**

On 28 May Bouncy Ltd, School Street, Wexford returned 2 faulty travel cots (faulty netting) at €72 each to Baby Supplies Ltd, Castle Street, Thurles. Trade discount is 20% and VAT is 10%. Draft the credit note sent by Baby Supplies Ltd on 28 May.

CREDIT NOTE
No.: 85

Baby Supplies Ltd
Castle Street
Thurles

Date: _____

_____

_____   Your Invoice No.: _____

_____

Quantity	Description	Code	Price Each	Total €
			Total (excluding VAT)	
			Trade discount	
			Subtotal	
			VAT	
			Total (including VAT)	

E & O E

17 Tick (✓) whether each of the following is true or false:

	TRUE	FALSE
The supplier sends the letter of enquiry		
The customer sends the invoice		
The supplier sends the credit note		

On 22 June Digital Supplies Ltd, Great Water Industrial Estate, Longford, sent an invoice, no. 418, to Techie Ltd, Blackhall Street, Mullingar for the following goods: 12 cameras (C42) at €64 each, 15 22" flat screen TVs (FTV22) at €172 each and 9 mini camcorders (MC16) at €59 each. Trade discount is 20% and VAT is 10%. Draft the invoice sent on 22 June.

INVOICE

No.: 418

Digital Supplies Ltd
Great Water Industrial Estate
Longford

Date: _____

_____

_____

_____

Quantity	Description	Code	Price Each	Total €
		Total (excluding VAT)		
		Trade discount		
		Subtotal		
		VAT		
		Total (including VAT)		

E & O E

---

19 Fill in the two blank spaces to show the sequence of documents used when purchasing goods.

Letter of Enquiry	→		→	**Order**	→	

On 30 June Techie Ltd, Blackhall Street, Mullingar returned 2 faulty cameras (faulty lens) at €64 each to Digital Supplies Ltd, Great Water Industrial Estate, Longford. Trade discount is 20% and VAT is 10%. Draft the credit note sent by Digital Supplies Ltd on 1 July.

CREDIT NOTE

No.: 235

Digital Supplies Ltd
Great Water Industrial Estate
Longford

Date: _____

Your Invoice No.: _____

Quantity	Description	Code	Price Each	Total €

Total (excluding VAT)	
Trade discount	
Subtotal	
VAT	
Total (including VAT)	

E & O E

---

21 How does a shop know whether to give credit to a customer or insist on cash?

....

....

....

....

On 8 July Scooter Supplies Ltd, Swords, Co. Dublin, sent an invoice, no. 517, to Lucan Bikes Ltd, Main Street, Lucan for the following goods: 30 helmets (H62) at €46 each, 15 biker pants (BP32) at €38 each and 20 motorbike jackets (MJ48) at €43 each. Trade discount is 20% and VAT is 10%. Draft the invoice sent on 8 July.

INVOICE

No.: 517

Scooter Supplies Ltd
Swords
Co. Dublin

Date: _____

Quantity	Description	Code	Price Each	Total €

Total (excluding VAT)	
Trade discount	
Subtotal	
VAT	
Total (including VAT)	

E & O E

On 12 July Lucan Bikes Ltd, Main Street, Lucan returned 2 faulty helmets (faulty straps) at €46 each to Scooter Supplies Ltd, Swords, Co. Dublin. Trade discount is 20% and VAT is 10%. Draft the credit note sent by Scooter Supplies Ltd on 13 July.

CREDIT NOTE

No.: 295

Scooter Supplies Ltd
Swords
Co. Dublin

Date:

Your Invoice No.:

Quantity	Description	Code	Price Each	Total €
			Total (excluding VAT)	
			Trade discount	
			Subtotal	
			VAT	
			Total (including VAT)	

E & O E

24 What is meant by 'stock control'?

....

....

....

....

Seller: Bath Supplies Ltd, Main Street, Athlone.
Buyer: BrayBuild Ltd, Seaview Avenue, Bray, Co. Wicklow.

On 1 April, BrayBuild Ltd owed Bath Supplies Ltd €3,500.

The following transactions took place during the month of April.
    10 April   Bath Supplies Ltd received a cheque from BrayBuild Ltd for €1,800.
    15 April   Bath Supplies Ltd sent an invoice no. 43 to BrayBuild Ltd, €6,000 + VAT 20%
    24 April   Bath Supplies Ltd sent a credit note no. 28 to BrayBuild Ltd, €1,300 + VAT 20%

From the above details, complete the statement no. 59.

STATEMENT
No.: 59

Bath Supplies Ltd
Main Street
Athlone

Date:

_____

_____

_____

Date	Details	Debit	Credit	Balance

26 What should a customer do when a statement is received?

....

....

....

....

Seller: Carco Ltd, Castle Street, Carlow.
Buyer: Donegal Garage Ltd, Killybegs Avenue, Donegal.

On 1 May, Donegal Garage Ltd owed Carco Ltd €2,600.

The following transactions took place during the month of May.
- 11 May   Carco Ltd sent an invoice no. 289 to Donegal Garage Ltd, €3,500 + VAT 20%
- 18 May   Carco Ltd received a cheque from Donegal Garage Ltd for €2,200.
- 24 May   Carco Ltd sent a credit note no. 124 to Donegal Garage Ltd, €900 + VAT 20%

From the above details, complete the statement no. 317.

STATEMENT

No.: 317

Carco Ltd
Castle Street
Carlow

Date:

_____
_____
_____

Date	Details	Debit	Credit	Balance

28 Tick (✓) whether each of the following is true or false:

	TRUE	FALSE
The supplier sends the invoice		
The supplier sends the credit note		
The supplier sends the statement		

Seller: A1 Supplies Ltd, Main Street, Athlone.
Buyer: KerryBooks Ltd, Seaview Avenue, Co. Kerry.

On 1 June, KerryBooks Ltd owed A1 Supplies Ltd €1,800.

The following transactions took place during the month of June.
15 June A1 Supplies Ltd sent an invoice no. 241 to KerryBooks Ltd, €4,300 + VAT 20%
24 June A1 Supplies Ltd sent a credit note no. 97 to KerryBooks Ltd, €800 + VAT 20%
29 June A1 Supplies Ltd received a cheque from KerryBooks Ltd for €2,600.

From the above details, complete the statement no. 264.

STATEMENT

No.: 264

A1 Supplies Ltd
Main Street
Athlone

Date:

Date	Details	Debit	Credit	Balance

Patricia Blake works in the sales department of Time Wholesalers Ltd. On 10 March 2010, she receives an order, number 219, from Sarah Parsons, Dolmen Ltd, Department Store, 12-18 Main Street, Dundalk, for the following goods.

90	Men's Watches (WTM 74)	@ €40.00 each
70	Ladies' Watches (WTL 92)	@ €60.00 each
30	Alarm Clocks (CTA 58)	@ €26.50 each
80	Digital Watches (WCD 36)	@ €22.50 each

The goods ordered are in stock, except for the alarm clocks. All the other items (men's watches, ladies' watches and digital watches) are available.

From the above details, complete the invoice no. 1477 sent on 11 March 2010. Note that trade discount on all the goods is 15% and VAT on all the goods is 20%.

INVOICE
No.: 1477

Time Wholesalers Ltd
High Street
Waterford

Date: _____
Your Order No.: _____

Quantity	Description	Code	Price Each	Total €
			Total (excluding VAT)	
			Trade discount	
			Subtotal	
			VAT	
			Total (including VAT)	

E & O E

On 28 May 2010, Bright Paints Ltd, Décor Avenue, Brush Row, Galway received an order no. 3 from Martin Ltd, 10 Green Valley, Loughrea, Co. Galway for the following goods:

50	Ten-litre drums of white paint (WHP126)	@ €60 per drum
50	Five-litre drums of cream paint (CP75)	@ €80 per drum
15	Five-litre drums of wood preservative (WP63)	@ €50 per drum

All the goods ordered were in stock, except for the wood preservative.

Bright Paints Ltd issued invoice no. 42 for the goods in stock on 1 June 2010.

The invoice included the following terms: trade discount 30% and VAT 21%.

On receiving the goods and invoice no. 42 on 4 June 2010, Martin Ltd paid the amount due in full.

Bright Paints Ltd issued receipt no. 67, signed by Molly Bright, on 15 June 2010.

(i) What procedures would you recommend to Bright Paints Ltd when preparing and processing receipts?

(ii) Complete invoice no. 42 and receipt no. 67 issued by Bright Paints Ltd.

INVOICE

No.: 42

Bright Paints Ltd
Décor Avenue,
Brush Row, Galway

Date: _____

Your Order No.: _____

Quantity	Description	Code	Price Each	Total €

Total (excluding VAT)	
Trade discount	
Subtotal	
VAT	
Total (including VAT)	

Bright Paints Ltd Décor Avenue, Brush Row, Galway		No.: 67
Date:		
Received from:		
The sum of:		
		€
With thanks	Signed:	

The following details refer to the sale of goods on credit by Kenny Ltd, Main Street, Galway, to Brown Ltd, Claremorris, Co. Mayo for the month of April 2010.

On 1 April 2010, Brown Ltd owed Kenny Ltd €2,500.
The following transactions took place during the month of April.
10/4/2010 Kenny Ltd received a cheque no. 34 from Brown Ltd €1,750
23/4/2010 Kenny Ltd sent an invoice no. 22 to Brown Ltd ....€7,000 + VAT 21%
29/4/2010 Kenny Ltd sent a credit note no. 78 to Brown Ltd ....€1,800 + VAT 21%
On 30 April 2010, Kenny Ltd sent a statement of account no. 91 to Brown Ltd.

(i) Outline how Kenny Ltd should treat outgoing statements of account.
(ii) Complete the statement of account no. 91.

STATEMENT
No.: 91

Kenny Ltd
Main Street, Galway

Date:

_____

_____

_____

Date	Details	Debit	Credit	Balance

Martin Banner, Purchasing Manager of Homefit Ltd, Kilkee, Co. Clare, completed an order for 50 exterior teak doors (ETD27) @ €200 each and 100 interior pine doors (IPD24) @ €60 each from Joan Shannon, Doors for all Occasions Ltd, Wood Lane, Limerick. These were delivered on 18 May 2010. When Martin examined the doors, he found that 5 of the exterior teak doors were badly scratched. His complaint to Joan Shannon, Sales Manager, was accepted and she sent him a credit note no. 23 for the 5 exterior teak doors on 1 June 2010.
Trade discount is 20% and VAT is 21%.

Complete the credit note no. 23 issued on 1 June 2010.

CREDIT NOTE

No.: 23

Doors for all Occasions Ltd
Wood Lane
Limerick

Date:

Quantity	Description	Code	Price Each	Total €

Total (excluding VAT)	
Trade discount	
Subtotal	
VAT	
Total (including VAT)	

E & O E

eTest.ie
Try a test on this topic

1 Explain the term **Creditor**:

....

....

....

2 The following account appeared in the ledger of Eleanor Toomey.

Dr					**Ronnie Whelan Account**			Cr
Date	Details	F	Total	Date	Details		F	Total
			€					€
				May 17	Balance		b/d	500
				May 18	Purchases		PB	700

Complete the sentences below to explain the entries in the account.

On May 17, Toomey

....

....

On May 18, Toomey

....

....

3 From what source documents is the purchases returns day book written up?

Credit notes issued by the firm ☐

Credit notes received by the firm ☐

Copy of invoices issued ☐

(Tick (✓) the most appropriate box)

4 A firm had cash purchases of €120,000 (€100,000 + VAT €20,000) on 14 March. Record this in the accounts below.

Dr			Purchases Account				Cr
Date	Details	F	Total €	Date	Details	F	Total €
			VAT Account				
			Cash Account				

5 The following account appeared in the ledger of Jan Redmond.

Dr			Purchases Account				Cr
Date	Details	F	Total €	Date	Details	F	Total €
Apr 12	Bank	CB	12,000				
Apr 12	Sundry creditors	CB	23,000				

Complete the sentences below to explain the entries in the account.

On April 12, Redmond

....

....

On April 14, Redmond

....

....

Chapter 28

Sales and sales returns

1 Explain the term **Debtor**:

....

....

....

2 The following account appeared in the ledger of Bernard Warnock.

Dr				**Cathy Sullivan Account**			Cr
Date	Details	F	Total	Date	Details	F	Total
			€				€
Jun 1	Balance	b/d	800	Jun 7	Returns	SR	150

Complete the sentences below to explain the entries in the account.

On June 1, Warnock
....

....

On June 7, Warnock
....

....

3 A firm sells goods for €4,500. The cost of the goods was €2,800. Calculate the mark-up and the margin.

ANSWER	WORKINGS

4 A firm had cash sales of €60,000 (€50,000 + VAT €10,000) on 18 July. Record this in the accounts below.

Dr			Sales Account				Cr
Date	Details	F	Total	Date	Details	F	Total
			€				€

VAT Account

Cash Account

5 The following account appeared in the ledger of Niamh Moore.

Dr			Sales Account				Cr
Date	Details	F	Total	Date	Details	F	Total
			€				€
				Aug 21	Bank	CB	26,000
				Aug 22	Sundry debtors	CB	53,000

Complete the sentences below to explain the entries in the account.

On Aug 21, Moore

....

....

On Aug 22, Moore

....

....

Try a test on this topic

Chapter 29
Analysed *cash book*

Dr							Analysed Cash Book							Cr
Date	Details	F	Bank	Sales	VAT	Debtors	Capital	Date	Details	F	Bank	Purchases	VAT	Advertising
July			€	€	€	€	€	July			€	€	€	€
2	Capital		50,000				50,000	1	Balance	b/d	3,000			
6	Sales		24,000	20,000	4,000			8	Advertising	1	6,000			6,000
22	Bailey Ltd	3	5,000			5,000		27	Purchases	2	10,800	9,000	1,800	
								31	Balance	c/d	59,200			
			79,000	20,000	4,000	5,000	50,000				79,000	9,000	1,800	6,000
Aug 1	Balance		59,200											

1 Explain what each of these figures is in relation to the analysed cash book above.

€3,000	
€50,000	
€6,000	
€1,800	
€4,000	
€5,000	
€79,000	
€59,200	

2 Explain the term **Overheads**:

....

....

....

....

3 Record the following bank transactions for the month of June in the analysed cash book below.

Note: Analyse the bank transactions using the following money column headings:

Debit (Receipts) side: Bank; Sales; VAT; Debtors; Capital.

Credit (Payments) side: Bank; Purchases; VAT; Wages.

Jun 2   Shareholders invested €120,000 and this was lodged.

7   Cash sales lodged, €60,000 (€50,000 + €10,000 VAT).

9   Paid wages (cheque no. 1), €21,000.

23   Tobin Ltd paid €8,000 and this was lodged (receipt no. 3).

29   Purchases for resale (cheque no. 2), €40,000 + 20% VAT.

Analysed Cash Book

Dr

Date	Details	F	Bank	Sales	VAT	Debtors	Capital
			€	€	€	€	€

Cr

Date	Details	F	Bank	Purchases	VAT	Wages
			€	€	€	€

4 Record the following bank transactions for the month of June in the analysed cash book below.

Note: Analyse the bank transactions using the following money column headings:

Debit (Receipts) side: Bank; Sales; VAT; Debtors; Capital.

Credit (Payments) side: Bank; Purchases; VAT; Wages.

Jun 2   Shareholders invested €60,000 and this was lodged.

8   Purchases for resale (cheque no. 1), €18,000 + 20% VAT.

11   Paid wages (cheque no. 2), €29,000.

25   Fay Ltd paid €14,000 and this was lodged (receipt no. 1).

28   Cash sales lodged, €96,000 (€80,000 + €16,000 VAT).

Analysed Cash Book

Dr

Date	Details	F	Bank	Sales	VAT	Debtors	Capital
			€	€	€	€	€

Cr

Date	Details	F	Bank	Purchases	VAT	Wages
			€	€	€	€

5

Record the following bank transactions for the month of June in the analysed cash book below.
Note: Analyse the bank transactions using the following money column headings:

Debit (Receipts) side: Bank; Sales; VAT; Capital.
Credit (Payments) side: Bank; Purchases; VAT; Light and Heat; Creditors.

Jun 3   Shareholders invested €80,000 and this was lodged.

8   Paid light and heat (cheque no. 1), €2,000.

14   Cash sales lodged, €12,000 (€10,000 + €2,000 VAT).

26   Paid O'Donnell Ltd (cheque no. 2), €24,000.

29   Purchases for resale (cheque no. 3), €14,000 + 20% VAT.

eTest.ie — Try a test on this topic

Analysed Cash Book

Dr

Date	Details	F	Bank	Sales	VAT	Capital
			€	€	€	€

Cr

Date	Details	F	Bank	Purchases	VAT	Light and heat	Creditors
			€	€	€	€	€

Chapter 30

Petty cash book

Dr			Petty Cash Book								Cr
Date	Details	F	Total	Date	Details	F	Total	Motor	Postage	Stationery	Sundries
May			€	May			€	€	€	€	€
1	Balance	b/d	150	2	Paper	71	9			9	
				5	Postage	72	13		13		
				9	Envelopes	73	7			7	
				12	Petrol	74	43	43			
				15	Cleaning	75	25				25
				21	Motor oil	76	6	6			
				26	Postage	77	20		20		
				31	Balance	c/d	27				
			150				150	49	33	16	25
Jun 1	Balance		27								
	Bank		123								

1 Explain what each of these figures is in relation to the petty cash book above.

€150	
€9	
71	
€49	
€27	
€123	

2 Fergal Smith is an office manager. On June 7 he paid €35 for repairs to a printer. Enter the transaction in the petty cash voucher below.

Petty Cash Voucher No. 148

Date	
Details	Amount
Signature:	

3 Write up Fergal Smith's petty cash book for the month of July using the following analysis columns: Postage, Stationery, Repairs, Travel, Sundries.

Jul 1   Opening cash on hand, €400.

5   He bought writing paper (stationery) for €45 – Petty Cash Voucher No 76.

9   He paid €40 to a local charity – Petty Cash Voucher No 77.

12   He paid €62 for repairs to computer – Petty Cash Voucher No 78.

17   He paid €34 to Fast Couriers Ltd (postage) – Petty Cash Voucher No 79.

20   He paid €35 for cleaning of office – Petty Cash Voucher No 80.

26   He purchased printer paper (stationery) for €54 – Petty Cash Voucher No 81.

27   He paid train fare €55 for marketing manager – Petty Cash Voucher No 82.

31   He paid €24 for postage - Petty Cash Voucher No 83.

Petty Cash Book

Dr												Cr
Date	Details	F	Total	Date	Details	F	Total	Postage	Stationery	Repairs	Travel	Sundries
			€				€	€	€	€	€	€

4 Write up Jenny Madden's petty cash book for the month of August using the following analysis columns: Postage, Stationery, Cleaning, Repairs, Other.

Aug 1 Opening cash on hand, €350.
7 She paid €50 to a local charity – Petty Cash Voucher No. 57.
9 She paid €75 for cleaning of office – Petty Cash Voucher No. 61.
13 She bought envelopes (stationery) for €21 – Petty Cash Voucher No. 58.
16 She bought printer paper (stationery) for €38 – Petty Cash Voucher No. 63.
22 She paid €40 to the window cleaner – Petty Cash Voucher No. 59.
24 She paid €45 for repairs to a fax machine – Petty Cash Voucher No. 60.
27 She bought paper (stationery) for €26 – Petty Cash Voucher No. 56.
29 She paid €12 to post a parcel – Petty Cash Voucher No. 62.

Petty Cash Book

Dr											Cr
Total	F	Details	Date	F	Details	Date	Total	Postage	Stationery	Cleaning	Repairs	Other
€							€	€	€	€	€	€

5 Write up Hilda Kelly's petty cash book for the month of September using the following analysis columns: Postage, Stationery, Cleaning, Repairs, Other.

Sep 1 Opening cash on hand, €300.
4 She bought writing paper (stationery) for €11 – Petty Cash Voucher No. 56.
7 She paid €20 to a local charity for raffle tickets – Petty Cash Voucher No. 57.
9 She bought envelopes (stationery) for €18 – Petty Cash Voucher No. 58.
13 She paid €17 to the window cleaner – Petty Cash Voucher No. 59.
17 She paid €14 for repairs to a filing cabinet – Petty Cash Voucher No. 60.
24 She paid €25 for cleaning of office – Petty Cash Voucher No. 61.
26 She paid €8 to post a parcel to a customer – Petty Cash Voucher No. 62.
29 She bought printer paper (stationery) for €23 – Petty Cash Voucher No. 63.

Petty Cash Book

Dr					Cr					
Date	Details	F	Total	Date	Details	F	Total	Postage	Stationery	Cleaning	Repairs	Other
			€				€	€	€	€	€	€

1 On January 22, Office Supplies Ltd buys a new delivery van on credit from Salthill Garage Ltd, €18,000. Complete the general journal entry below to record this transaction in the books of Office Supplies Ltd.

	General Journal			
			Dr	Cr
Jan 22	Delivery van			
	Salthill Garage Ltd			
	Narration			

2 On February 14, Office Supplies Ltd sold an old delivery van on credit to John Quilligan, €2,000. Complete the general journal below to record this transaction in the books of Office Supplies Ltd.

	General Journal			
			Dr	Cr

3 On March 14, Ennis Bakery Ltd buys new office furniture on credit from Modern Interiors Ltd, €3,000. Complete the general journal below to record this transaction in the books of Ennis Bakery Ltd.

General Journal				
			Dr	Cr

4 On April 25, Ennis Bakery Ltd sold old office furniture on credit to Liz Hanley, €1,400. Complete the general journal below to record this transaction in the books of Ennis Bakery Ltd.

General Journal				
			Dr	Cr

5 On May 17, PC Tec Ltd, a computer manufacturer, bought new machinery on credit from Gahan Ltd, €120,000. Complete the general journal below to record this transaction in the books of PC Tec Ltd.

General Journal				
			Dr	Cr

General Journal

		Dr	Cr
	Buildings	400,000	
	Loan		100,000
	Share capital		300,000
	Assets, liabilities and capital on 1 January	400,000	400,000

1 Study the general journal above and answer these questions.

Name one asset in this firm:

....

Name one liability in this firm:

....

How much did the owners invest in the firm?

....

2 Calculate the share capital for this firm below and then complete this general journal.

General Journal

		Dr	Cr
	Buildings	550,000	
	Loan		150,000
	Share capital		
	Assets, liabilities and capital on 1 January		

3 A firm has the following assets and liabilities:

	€
Buildings	430,000
Loan	200,000

Complete the general journal below to record this and calculate the share capital.

General Journal			
		Dr	Cr
	Buildings		
	Loan		
	Share capital		
	Assets, liabilities and capital on 1 January		

4 A firm has the following assets and liabilities:

	€
Buildings	370,000
Debtor: J. Smith	26,000
Bank overdraft	80,000

Complete the general journal below to record this and calculate the share capital.

General Journal			
		Dr	Cr
	Buildings		
	Debtor: J. Smith		
	Bank overdraft		
	Share capital		
	Assets, liabilities and capital on 1 January		

General Journal

	Dr	Cr
Buildings	600,000	
Debtor: J. Smith	50,000	
Creditor: H. Stewart		20,000
Loan		200,000
Share capital		430,000
Assets, liabilities and capital on 1 January	650,000	650,000

5 Post the balances in the above general journal to the relevant ledger accounts below.

Buildings Account

Dr							Cr
Date	Details	F	Total	Date	Details	F	Total
			€				€

J. Smith Account

Date	Details	F	Total	Date	Details	F	Total

H. Stewart Account

Date	Details	F	Total	Date	Details	F	Total

Loan Account

Date	Details	F	Total	Date	Details	F	Total

Share Capital Account

Date	Details	F	Total	Date	Details	F	Total

Purchases Day Book

		Net	VAT	Total
Oct 7	Keevneys Ltd	8,000	1,680	

Sales Day Book

Oct 9	Cassidys Ltd	12,000	2,520	

6 Complete the total column in the sales and purchases day books above and then post the relevant figures from the day books to the ledger below.

Dr			Sales Account				Cr
Date	Details	F	Total	Date	Details	F	Total
			€				€

Purchases Account

VAT Account

Keevneys Ltd Account

Cassidys Ltd Account

Analysed Cash Book

Dr															Cr
Date	Details	F	Bank	Sales	VAT	Debtors	Capital	Date	Details	F	Bank	Purchases	VAT	Advertising
July			€	€	€	€	€	July			€	€	€	€
2	Capital		50,000				50,000	1	Balance	b/d	3,000			
6	Sales		24,000	20,000	4,000			8	Advertising	1	6,000			6,000
22	Bailey Ltd	3	5,000			5,000		27	Purchases	2	10,800	9,000	1,800	
								31	Balance	c/d	59,200			
			79,000	20,000	4,000	5,000	50,000				79,000	9,000	1,800	6,000
Aug 1	Balance		59,200											

7. Post the relevant figures from the cash book to the ledger below.

Dr							Cr
			Sales Account				
Date	Details	F	Total	Date	Details	F	Total
			€				€

			Purchases Account				

			VAT Account				

			Capital Account				

			Advertising Account				

			Bailey Ltd Account				

8 Balance the following VAT account.

Dr			VAT Account				Cr
Date	Details	F	Total	Date	Details	F	Total
			€				€
Mar 30	Sundry Creditors	PB	1,540	Mar 30	Sundry Debtors	SB	2,360

9 A firm has the following account balances in the ledger:

	€
Buildings	420,000
Machinery	260,000
Creditor: Keane Ltd	74,000
Cash	5,000
Purchases	120,000
Sales	431,000
Share Capital	300,000

Try a test on this topic

Using the above information, extract a the trial balance.

Trial Balance		Dr	Cr
Buildings			
Machinery			
Creditor: Keane Ltd			
Cash			
Purchases			
Sales			
Share Capital			

Chapter 33
Presentation of
ledger accounts

Dr			Bank Account			Cr	
Date	Details	F	Total	Date	Details	F	Total
			€				€
May 1	Balance	b/d	420	May 11	Advertising	CL	500
May 9	Sales	SB	1,800	May 16	Insurance	CL	840

1 Show the above account in the continuous balance format below.

	Bank Account					
Date	Details	F	Dr	Cr	Balance	
			€	€	€	
May 1	Balance				420	
May 9	Sales	SB				
May 11	Advertising	CL				
May 16	Insurance	CL				

Kevin Dillon's Account					
Date	Details	F	Dr	Cr	Balance
			€	€	€
Jun 1	Balance				560
Jun 5	Purchases	PB		410	970
Jun 7	Bank	CB	680		290

2 Show the above account in the traditional 'T' format below.

Dr				Kevin Dillon's Account			Cr
Date	Details	F	Total	Date	Details	F	Total
			€				€

Dr							Cr
Date	Details	F	Total	Date	Details	F	Total
			€				€
May 4	Sales	SB	540	May 1	Balance	b/d	280
				May 7	Rent	CL	600

3 Show the above account in the continuous balance format below.

Bank Account					
Date	Details	F	Dr	Cr	Balance
			€	€	€
May 1	Balance				(280)
May 4	Sales	SB			
May 7	Rent	CL			

Dr							Cr
Date	Details	F	Total	Date	Details	F	Total
			€				€
May 1	Balance	b/d	170	May 9	Insurance	CL	850
May 5	Sales	SB	620				

4 Show the above account in the continuous balance format below.

Bank Account					
Date	Details	F	Dr	Cr	Balance
			€	€	€
May 1	Balance				170
May 5	Sales	SB			
May 9	Insurance	CL			

Tina Brady 's Account					
Date	Details	F	Dr	Cr	Balance
			€	€	€
Jun 1	Balance				930
Jun 8	Purchases	PB		860	1,790
Jun 11	Bank	CB	750		1,040

5 Show the above account in the traditional 'T' format below.

Dr			Tina Brady's Account				Cr
Date	Details	F	Total	Date	Details	F	Total
			€				€

1 From the following information complete and balance the debtors' control account for the month of March:

Total credit sales for March, €17,000
Total cash received from debtors, €9,600
Total sales returns, €1,400

Dr				Debtors' Control Account			Cr
Date	Details	F	Total	Date	Details	F	Total
			€				€

2 From the following information complete and balance the creditors' control account for the month of April:

Total credit purchases for April, €6,800
Total cash paid to creditors, €5,100
Total purchases returns, €300

Dr				Creditors' Control Account			Cr
Date	Details	F	Total	Date	Details	F	Total
			€				€

3 From the following information complete and balance the debtors' control account for the month of May:

        Total credit sales for May, €45,000

        Total cash received from debtors, €38,000

        Total sales returns, €5,000

Dr			Debtors' Control Account				Cr
Date	Details	F	Total	Date	Details	F	Total
			€				€

4 From the following information complete and balance the creditors' control account for the month of June:

        Total credit purchases for June, €36,000

        Total cash paid to creditors, €29,000

        Total purchases returns, €4,000

Dr			Creditors' Control Account				Cr
Date	Details	F	Total	Date	Details	F	Total
			€				€

Try a test on this topic

1 From the following information prepare a trading account for the year ended 31 December.

	€
Sales	60,000
Opening stock	8,000
Purchases	32,000
Carriage in	5,000
Closing stock	9,000

Trading Account for the year ended 31 December				
		€	€	€
Sales				
Less cost of sales				
Opening stock				
+ Purchases				
+ Carriage in				
− Closing stock				
GROSS PROFIT				

2 From the following information prepare a trading account for the year ended 31 December.

	€
Sales	140,000
Opening stock	18,000
Purchases	83,000
Carriage in	6,000
Closing stock	16,000

Trading Account for the year ended 31 December				
		€	€	€
Sales				
Less cost of sales				
Opening stock				
+ Purchases				
+ Carriage in				
− Closing stock				
GROSS PROFIT				

Try a test on this topic

Chapter 36
Profit and loss account

1 From the following information prepare a profit and loss account for the year ended 31 December.

	€
Gross profit	103,000
Wages	63,000
Carriage out	4,000
Advertising	7,000
Electricity	3,000

Profit and Loss Account for the year ended 31 December				
		€	€	€
Gross profit				
Less expenses				
Wages				
Carriage out				
Advertising				
Electricity				
NET PROFIT				

2 For the above question, if sales were €220,000 calculate the gross profit percentage and the net profit percentage.

ANSWER	WORKINGS

3 From the following information prepare a trading and profit and loss account for the year ended 31 December.

	€
Cash sales	310,000
Opening stock	29,000
Cash purchases	265,000
Carriage in	3,200
Closing stock	27,600
Wages	92,000
Heating and lighting	11,000
Advertising	4,800
Carriage out	2,300
Dividend paid	25,000

Try a test on this topic

Trading, Profit and Loss Account for the year ended 31 December				
		€	€	€
Sales				
Less cost of sales				
Opening stock				
+ Purchases				
+ Carriage in				
− Closing stock				
GROSS PROFIT				
Less expenses				
Wages				
Heating and lighting				
Advertising				
Carriage out				
NET PROFIT				
Dividend				
RESERVE				

1. Vartry Ltd has 90,000 ordinary shares issued. Draft the appropriation account for the year ended 31 December given the following information.
   - Net profit is €34,000.
   - Last year's reserve (profit and loss balance) was €12,000.
   - Dividends declared are 10%.

		€	€	€
Profit and Loss Appropriation Account for the year ended 31 December				
	NET PROFIT			
	+ last year's reserve			
	− dividend			
	RESERVE			

2. Slaney Ltd has 120,000 ordinary shares issued. Draft the appropriation account for the year ended 31 December given the following information.
   - Net profit is €42,000.
   - Last year's reserve (profit and loss balance) was €7,000.
   - Dividends declared are 10%.

		€	€	€
Profit and Loss Appropriation Account for the year ended 31 December				
	NET PROFIT			
	+ last year's reserve			
	− dividend			
	RESERVE			

3 Shannon Ltd has 250,000 ordinary shares issued. From the following information prepare a trading, profit and loss and appropriation account for the year ended 31 December.

	€
Cash sales	530,000
Opening stock	32,000
Cash purchases	317,000
Carriage in	4,100
Closing stock	29,400
Wages	168,000
Heating and lighting	18,000
Insurance	6,000
Carriage out	3,700

Last year's reserve (profit and loss balance) was €18,000

Dividends declared are 10%

Try a test on this topic

Trading, Profit and Loss and Appropriation for the year ended 31 December			
	€	€	€
Sales			
Less cost of sales			
Opening stock			
+ Purchases			
+ Carriage in			
- Closing stock			
GROSS PROFIT			
Less expenses			
Wages			
Heating and lighting			
Insurance			
Carriage out			
NET PROFIT			
Last year's reserve			
Dividend			
RESERVE			

Chapter 38

Balance *sheet*

1 From the following information complete the balance sheet as at 31 December.

	€
Premises	250,000
Equipment	80,000
Closing stock	60,000
Cash on hand	4,000
Bank overdraft	35,000
Issued share capital	350,000
Reserve (profit and loss balance)	9,000

Balance Sheet as at 31 December				
		€	€	€
Fixed assets				
Premises				
Equipment				
Current assets				
Closing stock				
Cash on hand				
Current liabilities				
Bank overdraft				
Financed by				
Issued share capital				
Reserve				

2 From the following information prepare a trading, profit and loss and appropriation account for the year ended 31 December, and a balance sheet as at that date.

Trial balance as on 31 December

	€	€
Cash sales		340,000
Opening stock	20,000	
Cash purchases	170,000	
Carriage in	3,000	
Wages	64,000	
Heating and lighting	4,000	
Advertising	5,000	
Carriage out	3,000	
Dividend paid	25,000	
Motor vans	50,000	
Buildings	200,000	
Cash on hand	2,000	
Bank overdraft		6,000
Issued share capital		200,000
	546,000	546,000

Closing stock at 31 December is €25,000.

Trading, Profit and Loss and Appropriation for the year ended 31 December			
	€	€	€
Sales			
Less cost of sales			
Opening stock			
+ Purchases			
+ Carriage in			
− Closing stock			
GROSS PROFIT			
Less expenses			
Wages			
Heating and lighting			
Advertising			
Carriage out			
NET PROFIT			
Dividend			
RESERVE			

Balance Sheet as at 31 December			€	€	€
Fixed assets					
Motor vans					
Buildings					
Current assets					
Closing stock					
Cash on hand					
Current liabilities					
Bank overdraft					
Financed by					
Issued share capital					
Reserve					

3 For the trading, profit and loss and appropriation account on the previous page, calculate the gross profit percentage and the net profit percentage.

ANSWER	WORKINGS

4 From the following information complete the balance sheet as at 31 December.

	€
Motor vans	90,000
Buildings	140,000
Closing stock	60,000
Cash on hand	13,000
Bank overdraft	40,000
Issued share capital	260,000
Reserve (profit and loss balance)	3,000

Balance Sheet as at 31 December				
		€	€	€
Fixed assets				
Motor vans				
Buildings				
Current assets				
Closing stock				
Cash on hand				
Current liabilities				
Bank overdraft				
Financed by				
Issued share capital				
Reserve				

Try a test on this topic

Chapter 39

Final adjustments

1 Complete the electricity account below for the year ended 31 December 2010, showing the amount transferred to the final accounts on that date.

Note: There is no electricity due or prepaid at the end of the year.

Dr			Electricity Account					Cr
Date	Details	F	Total	Date	Details	F	Total	
			€				€	
Mar 1	Bank	CB	2,000	Jan 1	Balance	b/d	200	
Oct 1	Cash	CB	600					

2 Complete the insurance account below for the year ended 31 December 2010, showing the amount transferred to the final accounts on that date.

Note: There is €180 insurance prepaid at the end of the year.

Dr			Insurance Account					Cr
Date	Details	F	Total	Date	Details	F	Total	
			€				€	
Jan 1	Balance	b/d	150					
Mar 1	Bank	CB	720					

3 Complete the rent receivable account below for the year ended 31 December 2010, showing the amount transferred to the final accounts on that date.

Note: There is no rent receivable due or prepaid at the end of the year.

Dr	Rent Receivable Account						Cr
Date	Details	F	Total	Date	Details	F	Total
			€				€
Jan 1	Balance	b/d	100	Mar 1	Bank	CB	1,000
				Oct 1	Cash	CB	300

4 A company bought a van for €25,000. Depreciation is 20% per annum. Show the entry in the profit and loss account and the balance sheet.

Profit and Loss Account for year ended 31 December				
		€	€	€
	Expenses			

Balance Sheet as at 31 December				
		Cost €	Depr €	NBV €
	Fixed assets			

Try a test on this topic

1 The following trial balance was extracted from the books of Kelly Interiors Ltd on 31 December. The authorised share capital is 300,000 €1 ordinary shares.

Trial balance as on 31 December

	€	€
Purchases and sales	90,000	320,000
Purchases returns		3,000
Sales returns	4,000	
Opening stock	12,000	
Carriage in	1,000	
Wages	126,000	
Insurance	18,000	
Advertising	18,000	
Carriage out	2,000	
Rent receivable		17,000
Motor vans	60,000	
Buildings	320,000	
Debtors and creditors	35,000	14,000
Bank		7,000
15-year loan		100,000
Reserves (profit and loss)		25,000
Issued share capital		200,000
	686,000	686,000

You are required to prepare the company's trading, profit and loss and appropriation accounts for the year ending 31 December and a balance sheet as on that date. A template is provided on the next two pages.

You are given the following information:

(i)	Closing stock	15,000
(ii)	Rent receivable prepaid	3,000
(iii)	Advertising due	5,000
(iv)	Insurance prepaid	4,000
(v)	Dividends declared, 10%	
(vi)	Depreciation of vans, 20%	

Trading, Profit and Loss and Appropriation for the year ended 31 December

		€	€	€
Sales				
	Sales returns			
Cost of sales				
	Opening stock			
	Purchases			
	Purchases returns			
	Carriage in			
	Closing stock			
GROSS PROFIT				
Gains				
	Rent receivable			
Expenses				
	Wages			
	Insurance			
	Advertising			
	Carriage out			
	Depreciation of vans			
NET PROFIT				
	Last year's reserve			
	Dividend			
RESERVE				

	Balance Sheet as at 31 December			
		€	€	€
	Fixed assets			
	Motor vans			
	Buildings			
	Current assets			
	Closing stock			
	Debtors			
	Insurance prepaid			
	Current liabilities			
	Bank overdraft			
	Creditors			
	Rent receivable prepaid			
	Advertising due			
	Dividends due			
	Financed by			
	Authorised share capital			
	Issued share capital			
	Reserve			
	15-year loan			

2 Explain the term **Fixed Assets**:

....

....

....

....

....

3 List **three** expenses of a business:

   (i)
....

   (ii)
....

   (iii)
....

4 Tick (✓) whether each of the following is true or false:

	TRUE	FALSE
Sales are an expense of a business.		
The balance sheet lists things a firm owns and money it owes.		
Creditors is a current asset of a firm.		
Carriage in is shown in the trading account.		
Advertising is an expense of a firm.		

5 Explain the term **Share Capital**:

....

....

....

....

eTest.ie
Try a test on this topic

The directors of Palm Beach Ltd supplied the following information:

	€
Sales	400,000
Cost of sales	150,000
Average stock	14,000
Total expenses	180,000
Dividend paid	40,000
Issued share capital	300,000

1 Using the above information, calculate the following ratios:

Rate of stock turnover

....

....

Gross profit percentage

....

....

Net profit percentage

....

....

Total expenses as a percentage of sales

....

....

Rate of dividend

....

....

The directors of Jimmz Ltd supplied the following information:

	€
Average stock	26,000
Net profit	90,000
Cost of sales	50,000
Dividend paid	20,000
Current liabilities	36,000
Current assets	82,000
Issued share capital	160,000
Capital employed	280,000

2 Using the above information, calculate the following ratios:

Rate of stock turnover

....

....

....

Rate of dividend

....

....

....

Return on capital employed

....

....

....

Current ratio

....

....

....

3 Explain the term **Overtrading.**

....

....

....

Trading, Profit and Loss Account for the year ended 31 December		€	€
Sales			400,000
Less cost of sales			
Opening stock		20,000	
+ Purchases		240,000	
		260,000	
- Closing stock		30,000	
Cost of sales			230,000
GROSS PROFIT			**170,000**
Total expenses			90,000
NET PROFIT			**80,000**
Less dividend			30,000
Reserve			**50,000**

4 Using the above information, calculate the following ratios:

Rate of stock turnover

....

....

....

Gross profit percentage

....

....

....

Net profit percentage

....

....

....

Total expenses as a percentage of sales

....

....

....

Rate of dividend, if the issued share capital is €360,000

....

....

....

Balance sheet as at 31 December			€	€
Fixed assets				680,000
Current assets (including closing stock, €110,000)		270,000		
Current liabilities		150,000		120,000
				800,000
Financed by				
Issued share capital				550,000
Reserve				200,000
Term loan				50,000
				800,000

5 Using the above information, calculate the following ratios:

Working capital ratio

....

....

....

Acid test (quick) ratio

....

....

....

Return on capital employed, if the net profit is €80,000

....

....

....

6 Explain the term **Solvent**.

....

....

....

Try a test on this topic

Dr													Cr
Analysed Receipts and Payments Account													
Date	Details	F	Total	Subs	Competitions	Disco	Date	Details	F	Total	Wages	Competitions	Disco
Jul			€	€	€	€	Jul			€	€	€	€
1	Balance	b/d	400				8	Prizes	400	50		50	
7	Subs		80	80			14	DJ	401	150			150
9	Entry fees		120		120		21	Caretaker	402	300	300		
11	Disco		350			350	23	Prizes	403	70		70	
17	Subs		80	80			29	Caretaker	404	300	300		
25	Entry fees		250		250		31	DJ	405	150			150
28	Disco		450			450	31	Balance	c/d	710			
			1,730	160	370	800				1,730	600	120	300
Aug 1	Balance		710										

1 Explain what each of these figures is in relation to the receipts and payments account above.

€400	
€150	
€160	
€1,730	
€710	
€1,020	

2 List **three** items that are contained in the treasurer's report:

(i)
....

(ii)
....

(iii)
....

3 On 1 June 2009, Gracefield Tennis Club had the following assets and liabilities:

Land €260,000; Equipment €200,000; Term Loan €50,000; Cash €3,000.

The following is a summary of the club's financial transactions for the year ended 31 May 2010:

Receipts:	**€**
Competition Fees	45,800
Subscriptions	74,300
Annual Sponsorship	20,000

Payments:	**€**
Repairs	2,800
Stationery	1,600
Wages	32,800
Competition Expenses	6,900
Insurance	4,730
Purchase of Land	16,500

Additional information at 31 May 2010:
(i) Subscriptions prepaid €2,400.
(ii) Stationery on hand €350.
(iii) Wages due €700.
(iv) Depreciation:
Equipment 15% of €200,000.

Prepare:
(i) A statement calculating the club's accumulated fund.
(ii) Receipts and payments account.
(iii) Income and expenditure account.

Accumulated Fund					
					€
	Land				
	Equipment				
	Cash				
	Term loan				
	Accumulated Fund				

Dr				Receipts and Payments Account				Cr
Date	Details	F	Total	Date	Details	F		Total
			€					€
Jun 1	Balance	b/d	3,000	Jun 1	Repairs			
	Competition fees				Stationery			
	Subscriptions				Wages			
	Sponsorship				Competition exp			
					Insurance			
					Land			

Income and Expenditure Account for year ended 31 December					
			€	€	€
	Income				
	Competition profit				
	Subscriptions				
	Annual sponsorship				
	Expenditure				
	Repairs				
	Stationery				
	Wages				
	Insurance				
	Depreciation of equipment				
	Surplus				

eTest.ie
Try a test on this topic

Given the following information, write up and balance the analysed receipts and payments account of the Boyne Golf Club for the month of July. (All dealings are in cash.)

July 1   Cash on hand since last month, €550
7   Received annual subscriptions from members, €90
8   Paid competition prizes, €60 (cheque no. 400)
9   Received competition entry fees, €150
17   Received annual subscriptions from members, €90
21   Paid caretaker's wages, €250 (cheque no. 402)
23   Bought prizes for next competition, €40 (cheque no. 403)
25   Received competition entry fees, €6 each from 50 members
28   Disco night: received €350 at the door.
29   Paid caretaker's wages, €250 (cheque no. 404).
31   Paid DJ €160 for running the disco (cheque no. 405)

Analysed Receipts and Payments Account

Dr

Date	Details	F	Total	Subs	Competitions	Disco
			€	€	€	€

Cr

Date	Details	F	Total	Wages	Competitions	Disco
			€	€	€	€

Chapter 43
Farm *accounts*

Dr						Analysed Receipts and Payments Account						Cr
Date	Details	F	Total	Cattle	Grants	Date	Details	F	Total	Cattle	Feed	Other
May			€	€	€	May			€	€	€	€
1	Balance	b/d	2,000			7	Cattle feed	711	800		800	
5	Cattle	401	7,500	7,500		10	Calves	712	3,800	3,800		
8	EU grant	402	3,000		3,000	15	Repairs	713	1,200			1,200
						28	Cattle feed	717	700		700	
						31	Balance	c/d	6,000			
			12,500	7,500	3,000				12,500	3,800	1,500	1,200
Aug 1	Balance	b/d	6,000									

1 Explain what each of these figures is in relation to the receipts and payments account above.

€2,000	
€7,500	
€800	
€1,200	
€1,500	
€6,000	

2 Tick (✓) the most suitable type of finance/loan for each of the following items required by a farmer.

Items	Type of loan		
	Short term	Medium term	Long term
Land			
Equipment			
Feed for cattle			
Diesel for tractor			

3 Given the following information, write up and balance the analysed receipts and payments account of Leo Sutton for the month of May. (All dealings are in cash.)

May 1	Balance in bank, €3,700
5	Sold cattle for €12,500 (receipt no. 501)
7	Purchased cattle feed for €800 (cheque no. 711)
8	Received an EU grant of €3,600 (receipt no. 502)
10	Purchased cattle (calves) for €2,600 (cheque no. 712)
15	Paid for repairs to tractor, €700 (cheque no. 713)
18	Paid fees to vet, €1,900 (cheque no. 714)
22	Purchased cattle (calves) for €3,400 (cheque no. 715)
24	Received a state grant of €1,000 (receipt no. 503)
26	Sold cattle for €16,500 (receipt no. 503)
27	Purchased diesel oil for machinery, €790 (cheque no. 716)

Analysed Receipts and Payments Account

Dr

Date	Details	F	Total	Cattle	Grants		Date	Details	F	Total	Cattle	Feed	Other
			€	€	€					€	€	€	€

Cr

4

Given the following information, write up and balance the analysed receipts and payments account of Pat Maloney for the month of June. (All dealings are in cash.)

June 1 Balance in bank €2,500
3 Sold cattle for €29,500 (receipt no. 401)
7 Sold cattle at the mart for €17,500 (receipt no. 401)
8 Purchased cattle feed for €1,850 (cheque no. 811)
11 Purchased cattle (calves) for €4,000 (cheque no. 812)
13 Paid for repairs to tractor €900 (cheque no. 813)
14 Purchased diesel oil for machinery €850 (cheque no. 814)
18 Paid fees to vet €680 (cheque no. 815)
21 Sold cattle at the mart for €12,500 (receipt no. 403)
23 Purchased cattle feed for €4,400 (cheque no. 816)
28 Received a state grant of €2,000 (receipt no. 404)

Analysed Receipts and Payments Account

Dr

Date	Details	F	Total	Cattle	Grants	Other
			€	€	€	€

Cr

Date	Details	F	Total	Cattle	Feed	Other
			€	€	€	€

5 Given the following information, write up and balance the analysed receipts and payments account of Jimmy Kennedy for the month of July. (All dealings are in cash.)

July 1	Balance in bank €5,200
3	Sold cattle for €16,500 (receipt no. 601)
7	Sold cattle at the mart for €13,500 (receipt no. 601)
8	Purchased cattle feed for €950 (cheque no. 711)
11	Purchased cattle (calves) for €2,800 (cheque no. 712)
13	Paid for repairs to tractor €700 (cheque no. 713)
14	Purchased diesel oil for machinery €930 (cheque no. 714)
18	Paid fees to vet €740 (cheque no. 715)
21	Sold cattle at the mart for €11,500 (receipt no. 603)
23	Purchased cattle feed for €4,800 (cheque no. 716)
28	Received a state grant of €3,000 (receipt no. 604)

Analysed Receipts and Payments Account

Dr

Date	Details	F	Total	Cattle	Grants	Other
			€	€	€	€

Cr

Date	Details	F	Total	Cattle	Feed	Other
			€	€	€	€

Chapter 44
Service *firms*

1 List **three** examples of service firms:

(i) ....

(ii) ....

(iii) ....

2 Explain the term **Operating Statement**:

....

....

....

....

3 List **three** reasons why a service company should keep accounts:

(i) ....

(ii) ....

(iii) ....

4 'Service firms have no stock.' Explain this statement.

....

....

....

....

5. From the following information prepare an operating statement for the year ended 31 December, and a balance sheet as at that date.

Trial balance as on 31 December

	€	€
Income from tours		55,000
Income from weddings		20,000
Income from daytime		32,000
Income from night-time		29,000
Secretary's wages	21,000	
Heating and lighting	4,000	
Advertising	6,000	
Petrol	25,000	
Insurance	18,000	
Vehicles	90,000	
Premises	170,000	
Cash on hand	6,000	
Bank overdraft		4,000
Issued share capital		200,000
	340,000	340,000

Operating Statement for year ended 31 December			
	€	€	€
Income			
Tours			
Weddings			
Daytime			
Night-time			
Expenditure			
Secretary's wages			
Heating and lighting			
Advertising			
Petrol			
Insurance			
Operating Profit			

Balance Sheet as at 31 December			€	€	€
Fixed assets					
Vehicles					
Premises					
Current assets					
Cash on hand					
Current liabilities					
Bank overdraft					
Financed by					
Issued share capital					
Operating profit					

6 Explain the term **Fixed Assets**:

....

....

....

....

7 Explain the term **Liabilities**:

....

....

....

....

Try a test on this topic

Given the following information, write up and balance the analysed receipts and payments account of Quick Deliveries Ltd for the month of September. (All dealings are in cash.)

Sep 1 Balance in bank, €2,000
3 Received €2,300 from Foleys Ltd (receipt no. 401)
7 Paid van driver's wages, €1,300 (cheque no. 811)
9 Received €800 from G. Byrne (receipt no. 402)
10 Paid for diesel, €240 (cheque no. 812)
13 Paid for repairs to van, €620 (cheque no. 813)
14 Paid van driver's wages, €1,300 (cheque no. 814)
18 Received €870 from C. Clancy (receipt no. 403)
24 Received €3,600 from Walsh Ltd (receipt no. 404)
26 Paid for office cleaning, €340 (cheque no. 816)
28 Paid van driver's wages, €1,300 (cheque no. 917)
29 Received €3,500 from Hortons Ltd (receipt no. 406)

Analysed Receipts and Payments Account

Dr

Date	Details	F	Total	Business	Domestic
			€	€	€

Cr

Date	Details	F	Total	Wages	Motor	Other
			€	€	€	€

Chapter 45
Information *technology*

1 Find the information technology terms hidden in this grid:

Disk ✓

Mouse

Display

Monitor

Modem

Ink

ROM

Laser

Scanner

RAM

Keyboard

```
D  C  A  N  R  A  O  B  Y  E  K
D  I  S  K  O  E  L  O  A  M  O
M  O  D  E  M  A  N  A  L  O  Y
O  A  Y  K  S  O  S  N  P  N  A
N  S  C  E  E  Y  U  S  A  I  L
I  O  R  A  M  S  O  S  E  C  P
T  K  D  R  A  O  B  Y  E  K  S
O  A  C  S  N  N  E  R  K  N  I
R  O  S  A  Y  E  K  O  A  R  D
```

2 Circle the input devices from the hardware listed below, as in the example.

Keyboard	Monitor
Mouse	Joystick
Disk drive	Printer
CD	Scanner

3 Column 1 is a list of abbreviations. Column 2 is a list of meanings which can be matched to these abbreviations. *(One description cannot be matched.)*

Column 1 Abbreviations	Column 2 Meanings
1. VDU	A. Controls the operation of the computer
2. RAM	B. Information here is lost when the machine is shut down
3. DVD	C. Can only be read
4. Kb	D. The computer's short-term memory
5. CPU	E. A way of controlling programs without using the keyboard
6. ROM	F. A way of measuring computer memory
	G. An output device

Match the two lists by placing the letter of the most appropriate description under the relevant number below:

1.	2.	3.	4.	5.	6.

4 Briefly describe each of the following business applications.

Word processor

....

....

....

....

Spreadsheet

....

....

....

....

Database

....

....

....

....

5 Find a word in the list to complete each word in the table:

Merge

Base

Ware

Sheet

Board

Spread	
Key	
Mail	
Data	
Hard	

6 Explain the function of a **Flash Drive**:

....

....

....

....

7 In each space below, write the most appropriate word or term from the following list:

DISK   MOUSE   RAM   SCANNER   LASER   ROM   KEYBOARD
(One of the words/terms above does not complete any of the sentences below.)

(i) A .... printer gives good quality hard copy.

(ii) The .... is the computer's short-term memory.

(iii) The QWERTY .... is used to type text into a computer.

(iv) A .... lets you use programs without using the keyboard.

(v) Use a .... to copy pictures into a computer.

(vi) You can use a .... drive as both an input and an output device.

8 Tick (✓) whether each of the following is true or false:

	TRUE	FALSE
A keyboard is an output device		
A printer is an output device		
A database is a computerised filing system		
A word processor is used to perform mathematical calculations		
The CPU is at the heart of a computer		

9 List **three** ways a computer can assist a business:

(i)
....

(ii)
....

(iii)
....

10 Distinguish between hardware and software.

Hardware
....

....

Software
....

....

eTest.ie
Try a test on this topic

11 On March 12, Office Furniture Ltd bought a new computer on credit from Tech World Ltd, €3,400. Complete the general journal below to record this transaction in the books of Office Furniture Ltd.

General Journal				
			Dr	Cr